Under none of the accredited ghostly circumstances, and environed
by none of the conventional ghostly surroundings, did I first make
acquaintance with the house which is the subject of this piece. I saw it in
the daylight, with the sun upon it. There was no wind,
no rain, no lightning, no thunder, no awful or unwonted
circumstance, of any kind, to heighten its effect.
The Haunted House by Charles Dickens

Happy Haunting
Jen Adams

Superstition, bigotry and prejudice, ghosts though they are, cling tenaciously to life; they are shades armed with tooth and claw. They must be grappled with unceasingly, for it is a fateful part of human destiny that it is condemned to wage perpetual war against ghosts. A shade is not easily taken by the throat and destroyed.
 Victor Hugo

You said I killed you - haunt me, then! The murdered do haunt their murderers, I believe. I know that ghosts have wandered on earth. Be with me always - take any form - drive me mad! only do not leave me in this abyss, where I cannot find you!
Emily Bronte

 It had grown darker as they talked, and the wind was sawing and the sawdust was whirling outside paler windows. The underlying churchyard was already settling into deep dim shade, and the shade was creeping up to the housetops among which they sat. "As if," said Eugene, "as if the churchyard ghosts were rising."
Charles Dickens

It is wonderful that five thousand years have now elapsed since the creation of the world, and still it is undecided whether or not there has ever been an instance of the spirit of any person appearing after death. All argument is against it; but all belief is for it.
Samuel Johnson

I look for ghosts; but none will force
Their way to me. 'Tis falsely said
That there was ever intercourse
Between the living and the dead.
William Wordsworth

Ghosts seem harder to please than we are; it is as though they haunted for haunting's sake - - much as we relive, brood, and smolder over our pasts.
Elizabeth Bowen

HAUNTED ILLINOIS SERIES

PHANTOMS IN THE LOOKING GLASS
HISTORY AND HAUNTINGS OF THE ILLINOIS PRAIRIE
BY LEN ADAMS

- A Whitechapel Productions Press Book from Dark Haven Entertainment -

ORIGINAL COVER ARTWORK DESIGNED BY
©Copyright 2008 by Michael Schwab & Troy Taylor
Visit M & S Graphics at http://www.manyhorses.com/msgraphics.htm

THIS BOOK IS PUBLISHED BY:
Whitechapel Press
A Division of Dark Haven Entertainment, Inc.
15 Forest Knolls Estates - Decatur, Illinois - 62521
(217) 422-1002 / 1-888-GHOSTLY
Visit us on the internet at http://www. dark haven entertainment. com

First Printing -- October 2008
ISBN: 1-892523-61-2

Printed in the United States of America

TABLE OF CONTENTS

SPECIAL THANKS

A book of this nature would never have come about if it were left up to me. So many people aided, guided, gathered information, or kicked me in the backside so that these wonderful tales would see the printed page.

Always the first person on my list to thank is Kim, my wife of 32 years (when the book comes out). She has guided, prodded, nagged, typed and assisted on every page of this work. Without her support and love I would've been content to let the world pass me by rather than grab hold and go for one incredible ride. I know I don't tell her enough, but I couldn't imagine my life without her.

I thank my wonderful children, Megan and Josh. Though you are both adults, I'll always see you with Kool-Aid around your mouths and peanut butter all over your hands. You've always been there for Dear Old Dad. I hope that I've always have been there for you.

Again, I thank my parents for having me. They've never said it but I know that I'm their favorite.

For the crazy assortment of goofballs I call my team: Julie, Luke, Bill and Matt. Thanks for letting the old guy hang around.

I also want to thank the collection of true friends I've made in Lebanon: Don, Gigi, Ernie, Mitz, Turnip, Jenifer, Chris, Bonnie, Harrison, Harriet, Linda, Lynda, Kathy, Janet, Sarah, Pat and Michelle. It's late in the day and I know I've missed a few. You guys make the journey a real blast.

Last, but certainly not least, I want to thank two special people. Troy Taylor, you've been a mentor, a guide, a drinking buddy and a cohort. But most of all you've been a friend. Thank you for all your support through the good and the bad times. I honestly believe the good times are here to stay.

Special thanks goes to my good friend and mentor, John Brill. Though John is no longer with us physically, he'll always live on in our hearts. When John passed away, those of us in the paranormal community who were close to him jumped at every noise we couldn't explain. We were sure it was John j saying goodbye.

Thanks to all of you out there who find my little tales of things that go bump in the night entertaining. That's all I've wanted to do, entertain you.

God bless, and as always, Happy Hauntings.
Len Adams
Summer 2008

INTRODUCTION

The fact that I am a published author is beyond my comprehension. I hate writing a grocery list! I thought a book would never be.

By the end of 2005, my good buddy, Troy Taylor, was struggling with his next endeavor. Troy wanted to do a sequel to his book, "Confessions of a Ghost Hunter."" At the time, his material would only get him halfway there.

One evening over several cocktails, I was regaling Troy (or boring him) with stories of my adventures in Alton and throughout Southern Illinois. With Troy's move back to Decatur, I was now the lead tour guide for his very successful "Alton Hauntings Tours." As an American Ghost Society rep, I was doing extensive investigations throughout the area. The tales weren't hard to come by and some of them were believable. Troy, unable to bear my sagas any longer, looked me in the eye and told me to write everything down. I informed him that I was a storyteller, not an author. He simply told me to tell my stories on paper.

So in 2006, my first book, "So There I Was: More Confessions of Ghost Hunters," came into being. As coauthor, I rode Troy Taylor's coattails to wildly successful reviews. Though my name was on the book, I still didn't consider myself an author.

As time passed and copies of our adventures flew off the bookshelves, I was told that the public wanted another piece of literature from me. I have the e-mails and letters. They really did!

By this time I had started the Haunted Lebanon tours in Lebanon, Ill. I was constantly telling Troy that I would match Lebanon against Alton, square foot by square foot, for ghostly activity. Again, unable to bear it any longer, he exclaimed, " All right big mouth, put up or shut up!" And the Haunted Lebanon tours were born.

I now had fodder for a second book. So there I was, and there it was. As 90 percent of the history of Lebanon is oral, I know there may be some of you who disagree with a fact here and there. It was like investigating a car accident. If 10 people see the same car wreck, there will be 10 different versions of the event. While sweating bullets over which tale to pick, a good friend of mine, Harrison Church, told me to grab the one I liked best and run with it. So that's what I did.

Some of the names and places were changed to protect the innocent and the drunk. The stories were collected over several years and they are told to the best of my ability.

All the tales of the paranormal are real, with real people. So curl up in your favorite chair with only a reading lamp on and discover what's on the other side of Lebanon.

Becoming a Ghost Hunter

If anyone had told me that at the ripe old age of 50, I would be a paranormal investigator, I would have told them they were batty!

Growing up, I had a love of horror flicks, not the garbage they spew out today, but the classics: "The Wolfman", "Dracula", "Frankenstein", the Hammer films and Vincent Price's Edgar Allan Poe flicks were my bill of fare. Unfortunately, there were repercussions. On many nights I lay in bed with the covers wrapped tightly around my body so the monsters couldn't get me. I was so afraid of the dark that when I had to go down the hallway to my room, I would carry my sister, Robin, who was three years younger, under my arm to feed her to the evil that I knew was waiting for me. My mother said I could turn off the light switch in the back of the house and be in the living room before the light went out. These were my early years.

Halloween, which is still my favorite holiday, held no terror for me, only candy! As a teenager I still loved horror films. Because I was older, they could be explained away as only something that Hollywood created, but then came "The Exorcist." Being

A 1961 photo of myself and my sister, Robin -- often referred to as "monster bait" for whatever was hiding in the shadows of our house.

raised Catholic and attending Catholic grade school in the '60s I was fed a steady stream of God's wrath and the evil all around us. Possession was a result of being bad, a punishment. I attended a showing of "The Exorcist" with a group of 20 of my friends. I didn't sleep for the next three nights! That demonic face still haunts me, as do my years of grade school. I've been able to overcome Catholic school, but not the face of evil.

I met my current wife, and she'll kill me if I don't say my only wife, two years after high school. Neither one of us had any money. We did have something more important though, we had love of the horror classics. There was a program in the mid-'70s on WSIU Carbondale, channel 9 on the old black and white TV. It was called "Monster Horror Theatre," hosted by Irv Coppi, and it was on every Friday night at 10 p.m. Kim and I, popcorn and soda at the ready, would lose ourselves in the classics. This passion and our two children have kept us together for more than 31 years. Despite this love of horror films, I still denied the possibility of something out there that was real, something legitimate.

Kim and I were married on October 16, 1976. On April 15, 1979, our daughter, Megan, was born. At this time my father-in-law, Bob, and his second wife, Doris, lived in a farmhouse in Okawville, Ill. This house, and the property around it, had been in Doris' family for many generations. On many a Saturday, Kim and I would load Megan in the car and travel the 25 miles to the old farmhouse. The days were spent working around the farm and the nights were spent at Original Springs Hotel. Dinner at the hotel always consisted of fried chicken with all the fixings. Of course, an ample amount of beer was needed to wash everything down. You don't grow up half Irish and half German and not drink beer. After dinner at the hotel, we would sit on the porch at the farmhouse and tell stories. On many nights, the stories would take a ghostly turn. Bob, Doris, and Doris' brother, Richard Baehr, who at the time lived next door, would tell us tales of the hauntings in the house and on the property. Bob, a draftsman, had fixed up one of the downstairs bedrooms as his office. Because he was his own employer, he could work whenever he wanted. On more than one occasion, Bob would be at the drafting table well into the night.

One night around midnight, Bob told us, he was working at the drafting table when a shadow moved across him and his workstation. For this to happen, someone, or something, would have had to move behind him and in front of the ceiling light. Of course, when he turned around, no one was there.

Richard had lived in the house until Bob and Doris moved in. Richard is a very down-to-earth, quiet individual. He'll speak up when he has something to say. If he doesn't, he's as quiet as a church mouse. During one of our ghost story sessions on the back porch, we were all stunned when Richard smiled and said that he had had a few strange experiences in the house. Now we were the quiet ones.

Richard said that while living alone in the house, he would hear footsteps upstairs, see doors opening and closing, and see shadows moving from room to room. He laughed when describing how the kitchen faucets seemed to have a life of their own.

Richard worked the many acres of the family farm. When Bob and Doris moved into the farmhouse, he bought a mobile home and moved it next door.

One evening, while walking toward the farmhouse, Richard saw a young girl sitting on the back porch steps. As he entered the yard through the back gate, he saw that the girl appeared to be in her late teens. She was clad in an old-fashioned white dress and had long curls in her hair. The young lady was sitting on the steps, crying. As Richard approached her, he asked if she was okay and whether she needed help.

A cracked old Polaroid photo of Bob and Doris' farm house near Okawville. Even this old photo doesn't look as creepy as the place actually was!

He said she lifted her face out of her hands, looked him the eyes, and simply vanished. When Doris asked why he never shared this story before now, Richard simply said, "I didn't think anyone would believe me."

Doris was the kindest, sweetest person you could ever meet. The sharpest criticism I can ever remember her making about someone was that a particular person was not very nice. Although sharing many of the same experiences as Bob and Richard, Doris tended not to speak about them as readily. She preferred a quieter approach to the problem. Doris had religious items spread throughout the house. The items didn't slow down the paranormal activity, but they made her feel better and more protected.

I, of course, never believed any of it. You need to know that I was born in Missouri, and the saying is true: "You have to show me for me to believe."

One Saturday in November 1979, after dinner and tall tales, we all retired for the night. Kim and I would sleep in the parlor on the hide-a-bed sofa. Megan would be in a bassinette next to us. What makes this night so frightening for me was what happened earlier that day.

During the mid-afternoon, I was helping Bob move some bedding and frames up to the second story, which consisted of two bedrooms on opposite sides of a long hallway. At the end of the hallway was a door that opened onto a balcony. Doris' daughters were coming for a visit and the bedrooms, which were normally empty, needed to be cleaned and furnished. Around 2 p.m., as I was assembling a bed frame in the hallway, I noticed Bob standing next to me. I thought it was Bob because I could see his legs. I kept rambling on about all we had to do, not letting it sink in that he wasn't responding to any of my questions. After a few minutes, I heard footsteps coming up the winding staircase that led to the second floor. This was to my left as I knelt on the floor. As the footfalls reached halfway up the staircase, I realized that they were coming from my father-in-law. Turning to my right, I saw a man wearing overalls and a dark shirt. He had a small beard, Amish in appearance, and graying hair. The expression on his face was one of anger. He had evidently been standing and staring at me the whole time. I turned to glance at Bob on the stairs. When I turned back to my right, the figure had vanished. My only thoughts were, what the hell was that? Not once was I scared. I didn't tell anyone what I had seen because I didn't want to appear as nutty as they were. By dinner time, this episode was forgotten.

Around midnight, as I lay in the hide-a-bed, I felt nature's call. Yes, I had had some beer at dinner, but not the usual gallon and a half that I normally drank. Nature's call was soon answered and, as I was washing my hands at the bathroom vanity, I looked into the medicine cabinet mirror. Standing behind me was the farmer I had seen earlier in the day! I spun around and there was no one there. Turning back to the mirror he was still there. Spinning around again, there was no one. Looking into the mirror a third time, he was gone.

Now he had my attention and now I was scared! I raced into the parlor and jumped into bed right up against Kim. Her response to my terror and need to be close was to inform me that it was too late and she wasn't in the mood.

This was the first, but far from the last episode I experienced in the farmhouse. Over the next two years, we would be witness to shadows moving across walls, disembodied voices, footsteps in empty rooms, and of course, the apparition of the farmer.

Another Saturday night, after our trip to the Original Springs Hotel for dinner, someone produced a Ouija board. I had never used one before and thought they were just a stupid game. When Bob suggested we use the board to try to contact the spirits in the house, I was all for it. I didn't believe that anything would actually happen, but what the heck... I was willing to give it a shot.

Bob and I sat down at the kitchen table with the planchette under our fingertips. After making each other swear that we wouldn't move it, we were ready to begin. Kim and Richard were seated on the other side of the table, pen and paper in hand, ready to record any answers we might get from the spirits. Doris was holding Megan and standing off to the side.

We started with the usual questions, such as is anybody here? How many? And so on. The planchette was going wild spelling out answers to our questions. At one point, Bob and I were staring at one another, each positive the other was moving the thing. As we did that, it continued to answer our questions. It wasn't us moving the planchette around. After 30 minutes of this, Bob asked if we could help the spirit in some way. That's when Doris grabbed the board off the table, ran out onto the porch and flung it into the yard.

"You never ask something like that," she screamed at us. "You're just inviting trouble!"

Whether we were or not, I didn't know. A name we picked up that night was Adam. On researching former owners of the property, we found a family that had a son by the name of Adam. Was it he who was haunting the property? What about the Amish-looking man and his wife? Yes, she started to appear also. Mostly they were seen in the detached summer kitchen. That's where Bob kept his tools for home repairs and projects. When he would ask me to go and get a wrench or hammer, I would tell him to get it himself. I was staying inside with everyone else.

Days and nights at the farmhouse were now taking a comical twist. No one wanted to be in the house by himself. A trip to the bathroom either brought a look of relief (literally) or one of surprise and confusion, as if in disbelief over something unexplained that had just happened. Even after the two upstairs bedrooms were finished, they were still used primarily for storage. Between Bob and Doris, they had collected a multitude of old books and magazines, along with quite a few antiques. Kim is an antique nut and I will read anything I can get my hands on. We would often go upstairs to wade amongst the treasures of the past, but never alone.

One spring day, Doris decided to organize the upstairs by putting the extra antiques in one bedroom and all the books and magazines in the other bedroom directly across the hall. That weekend during our normal visit, Kim and I decided to venture upstairs. It was 2 p.m. on a bright and beautiful day, what could happen?

Sunshine, warmth, and the sweet smell of honeysuckle drifting through the screened window greeted us on the upstairs landing. We smiled, thinking surely nothing could ruin this wonderful day. It didn't take long to note the changes that Doris had made. It wouldn't be a problem. The bedroom doors faced each other across the hall; we would leave them open so we could see one another. Nothing would ruin this adventure.

After about 10 minutes, I yelled across to the other room to see how Kim was doing. Receiving no reply, I turned to make my way across the hall. From the open doorway of my room, I could see Kim standing, transfixed in horror, as the door to her room was slowly closing under its own power. I would love to say that I made a mad dash for the closing door to save my wife. I would love to say that but it didn't happen that way. I casually walked over to the door, opened it, and then surveyed the room. The only thing that looked out of place was Kim. She was pale as a sheet and frozen to a spot in front of the window.

On questioning her, she said that she had a distinct feeling of being watched. Turning around, she saw the door, though propped open, start to close on its own. Now, I know what you're thinking: old house, old door, things settle and move on their own. I will agree with that, but this door was propped open. When it started to move, the doorstop that held it open was five feet away. The door came to a complete stop halfway through, and then started to move again before closing completely.

I opened the door without a problem and on further examination could find no reason for it to move on its own. It was hinged and weighted properly. It only opened and closed under someone's power.

We decided that this was a good time for a break. Surely someone would need our assistance downstairs.

About an hour later, I got the urge to return to the bedroom that held the treasure trove of books. Kim said that she would go, too, if I would stay close. We wandered around the antiques in the one bedroom, until the pull of the book room cast its spell on me. I slipped across the hall and into the other bedroom. Both doors were propped open to prevent their closing. Kim could see me, no problem.

After 20 to 30 minutes elapsed, I was sitting on the bedroom floor, lost in a book on ancient history. I assumed Kim realized that I was across the hall. As I went to check on her, I saw that the other bedroom door was closed again. I turned the knob and the door opened without a problem. Standing just on the other side of the door was Kim, tears in her eyes. "Where were you?" she screamed. I had to take her downstairs before she would calm down.

I asked her what had happened. Kim said that when she realized that I had left, the atmosphere of the room changed. Although it was warm outside, the bedroom had become icy cold. She knew it was time to leave. When she got five feet from the door, it slammed shut! Frantic, she pounded on the door and screamed for me. She said it seemed like an eternity before I showed up. Strangely, the entire time I was in the other room, I heard nothing. The only reason that I went to check on Kim was because I saw that the door was closed.

From that time on, any trips I made upstairs were made alone.

Unfortunately, whatever was haunting the upstairs bedrooms was not content to stay there. One night, after our usual dinner of chicken and beer at the Original Springs Hotel, Kim and I were hunkered down in the parlor in the hide-a-bed.

What was unique about this room was that in the old days, before funeral homes were in full use, people used to lay their deceased loved ones out for viewing in the living rooms or parlors of their homes. The room where we were sleeping had been used many times in this capacity. On this particular night, I slept (ironically) like a dead man. I don't think an exploding stick of dynamite could've woken me.

Around 1 a.m. Kim awoke with a start. She could hear the sound of footsteps marching through the rooms upstairs. This was nothing new; footsteps had been heard upstairs on a regular basis. To Kim though, these were different. The footfalls weren't of someone casually strolling around as they usually were. These were louder and more purposeful. Kim tried to wake me up to listen to the commotion upstairs. I was literally out cold. What happened next terrified her beyond imagination.

As the footsteps grew louder, Kim said she heard them leave the upstairs bedrooms and made their way down the hall. From there, they grew even louder as they descended the winding staircase into the room below. From that room to the parlor that held our bed was a distance of about 20 feet. The footsteps continued until they stopped at the foot of our bed. As if on cue, I immediately woke up and rolled over. There was Kim sitting upright in bed, eyes as big as fifty-cent pieces. It was becoming a habit in the old farmhouse for me to ask Kim what had happened. After she told me about the footsteps, I bravely decided that we should take Megan out of the crib next to our bed and let her sleep with us.

I eventually fell back to sleep, but by the look of Kim's eyes the next morning, she never did. That was one of the last nights we spent in the house. We had originally gone out on weekends to relax and unwind. We were now going home totally stressed out. Weekends in Okawville were now spent looking over our shoulders, waiting for something to happen.

In 1981, Bob and Doris moved to Phoenix, Ariz., and they told me that the window fan they had left at the farmhouse could be mine if I wanted it. All I had to do was go and get it. It was a warm and pleasant summer day. The house was vacant but I knew where to find the key. I had to work that day, which meant that I wouldn't get to the farmhouse until early evening. Because it was summer, with plenty of daylight, I thought this wouldn't be a problem.

Now, I've always been a fan of vampire films. But there is one thing in almost every one of them that drives me crazy. Why, when the hero wants to kill the vampire, and he knows where it is, does he wait until it's almost sundown to go and do the dirty deed? How stupid can he be? Why would you go and do something so terrifying when it's almost dark?

Instead of arriving at the farmhouse around 5:30 p.m., I met some friends at the hotel for a couple of beers before going to my destination. I wasn't killing vampires, but I was going alone into a haunted house. The house had electricity, but no permanent light fixtures. It was now 7:30 p.m. and the sun would be gone by 8:00.

So there I was...

And yes, I was now the stupid hero of my own ghost story. I entered through the rear of the house by way of the porch. From the porch, I would have to enter the kitchen, walk through the parlor, then go up the stairs to the second-floor bedroom that held my precious window fan in its clutches. Yes, this was the same bedroom with the cold spots and the magical door. But I knew I could do this and announced my intention to the house.

Just in case I needed to make a quick getaway, I left the kitchen and porch doors open. I made my way up the stairs and into the east bedroom. I now had 15 minutes of daylight left. No problem, I thought. The fan was propped in the window just waiting for me. I opened the window and grabbed the fan to sit it on the floor. When it wouldn't budge, I realized that it was screwed into the windowsill. Now what?

Luckily, I had a pocketknife with a screwdriver attachment so I set to work freeing my fan. Of course, I didn't know that the four screws holding my prize were three inches long! Halfway through the second screw, I realized that the room was now wrapped in shadows.

Sweat rolled down my forehead and my arms ached as I hurriedly kept working at the screws. Then a feeling came over me that I was no longer alone. At one point, as I felt someone directly behind me, I spun around and saw that the bedroom door was closed. This was the same door I had propped open to get some light from the west side of the house. I screamed, "I'm only here for the fan! Bob and Doris said I could have it!"

I don't remember if I removed the last two screws or just ripped the fan from the sill. I only remember slamming the window shut and running for the stairs. As anyone who's been on a ghost hunt with me will attest, I have no night vision. It hasn't gotten worse as I've aged; I never had it at all! This didn't stop me from hitting the stairs, fan clutched in my arms, at full speed. Miraculously, I made it down the stairs and into the kitchen. I made a sharp 90-degree turn to the right and ran smack dab into the now-closed kitchen door. As I got to my feet and picked up the fan, the water faucets in the sink somehow came on full blast.

I threw open the kitchen door and ran across the porch to my car. My heart was racing and I was drenched in sweat. I survived! I made it! But I forgot to lock up the house. As much as I wanted to leave, I had promised Bob I would make sure that everything was locked up good and tight. I usually have a pretty long stride when I walk, but now I was tiptoeing. I made it through the porch to the kitchen door. As I stepped in, I noticed the kitchen faucets weren't running anymore. I did remember to close the bedroom window, so I didn't have to go any farther. As I stepped from the kitchen to the porch, every water fixture in the house seemed to come alive. From the bathroom next to the kitchen, I could hear the toilet flush and the shower running. The kitchen faucets came back to life as I slammed the door and locked the deadbolt. As I turned to escape the watery hell, I almost fell into the cellar because its doors were now wide open! I leapt over the opening and ran to my car. As I sped away, I cursed my cheapness for wanting a free fan so desperately.

What makes a location become haunted? Is it due to a tragic death or another occurrence? Or can it be due to an imprint woven into the fabric of time? The farmhouse in Okawville seems to be in the perfect location for a residual, as well as an intelligent, haunting.

If a residual haunting is an imprint of the past that replays itself over and over, then the farmhouse and its surroundings are an ideal place for this to happen. The age of the farmhouse means that many have lived and died there. But the ground that the house sits on may hold a tale or two of its own. During our walks across the fields we would often come across Indian arrowheads and shards of pottery. Quite a community must have thrived there at one time. Also, the house is only a half-mile from the Kaskaskia River. Old homes, with their wells supplied by underground sources, and the river so close, are ripe spots for paranormal activity. Streams and underground waterways act as paranormal highways. For some reason, locations atop these "highways" are usually teeming with things that go bump in the night.

The house also seems to have its share of intelligent hauntings. From the Ouija board episode to the encounters with the bearded man and his wife, the spirits of the past interacted with the living.

During the mid-'80s, a new family moved into the farmhouse. The summer kitchen and back porch were torn down. I've talked to people who know the new owners and not one word has been said about ghosts. Possibly, by altering the house's configuration, all paranormal activity stopped. Another possibility is that the activity was connected to Doris, Richard, and their family because they were there for so long. Whatever the reasons are, I'll never forget the farmhouse for being my springboard into a lifelong quest for the answers that lie just beyond our reach.

In the years that followed, my interest in the paranormal took a backseat to the trials of everyday life. From the early '80s to the late '90s, Kim and I were occupied with two children, four residences, several jobs, and quite a few pets.

One October in the late 1990s, Kim told me about a haunted tour in Alton, Ill., hosted by Troy Taylor. I had been a reader of Troy's books for about a year and enjoyed then immensely. His "Haunted St. Louis" really held my interest. When he explained how violence often spawns a haunting and then used the old St. Louis gangs as an example, I was hooked. One of the gangs he wrote about was the Hogan Gang, led by Edward "Jellyroll" Hogan and his brother, James. They just happened to be my great uncles. The more I read, the more I realized that Troy knew as much about my family's past as I did. I had to meet this guy!

Not knowing how fast the tours sold out, I called for a reservation and learned that they had been sold out for quite some time. Fortunately for me, two people cancelled their Saturday reservations. When the night of the tour came I was really excited. I could actually go into some haunted locations with a lot of people. I would be scared, but thankfully, not alone. As Kim and I entered the History & Hauntings Bookstore, I was awestruck by the amount of books dealing with the paranormal. This was a ghost enthusiast's paradise!

Later, I would meet the store's owner, Bill Alsing. Bill bought History & Hauntings from Troy Taylor in 2004. He and I were to have many adventures together delving into the exciting world of paranormal investigations.

Before the tour, I got to meet the great man himself. Kim and I checked in with Troy as he stood behind the bookstore's counter. Not being able to control myself, I immediately started telling him about my connection to "Haunted St. Louis." The expression on his face was one of mild concern. Just great, he probably thought, another dingbat on the tour.

The tours at that time were on board a trolley. As much as I wanted to discuss all aspects of hauntings with Troy, it soon became apparent that so did everyone else. When the tour was over we were told about The American Ghost Society. The next day I spent several hours going over the website. I decided that this was indeed what I had been looking for. My quest would be to help unravel the mysteries of the paranormal. The game was afoot!

I became a member of The American Ghost Society. I eventually became an area rep, which soon led to my current position as vice-president of the organization. I can honestly say that it was one of the best happenings in my life. Troy is one of my best friends, ghost or no ghosts. Through Troy and the AGS, I've met so many wonderful people, and yes, some unique folks. I've worked with fellow enthusiasts from across the country, as well as England and Wales. I have the best investigative team in the world and I'd match them against anyone. I would march through the gates of hell with my people. (Of course, someone else would have to go first!) As the old saying goes, most people can count their true friends on one hand. Using both hands and feet wouldn't be enough to count the friends I've made in this field. I'm truly blessed in that respect.

It is often said that one man's trash is another man's treasure. Well, I also believe that one person's nightmare is another person's dream. And so it is with investigations of the paranormal. What is frightening and hair-raising to one can be a wealth of knowledge into another world for another.

In the winter of 1997, when I made my first trip to Lebanon, Ill., to audition for an upcoming community theater production of Neil Simon's comedy, "God's Favorite," I had no idea that another realm, an otherworldly realm, would soon envelope me.

My audition was stale and flat, as I hadn't been in the theater game for many years. Luckily, a fellow with more ego than talent turned down the small supporting role of the butler. I was called out of the bullpen to take up the challenge. As I had in the past, and still continue to do today, I took the part that was given to me and ran with it. Over the course of four weeks of rehearsals I kept adding my own warped and twisted interpretations of comedy and melded them into my character. I received enough attention, the good kind, that is, to continually get roles in wonderful productions over the years. I've worked my way from bit parts to leading roles, from janitorial duties to board president. Yes, Virginia, you do it all in community theater. You check your ego at the door and dive in enthusiastically to whatever needs to be done. This bonding of life with the local theater soon blossomed into a love affair with the town itself. An affair I hope to continue for the rest of my life.

The community of Lebanon is about ten miles northeast of Belleville, where I now reside. Because it's so close to home, numerous weekly trips are never a problem. Over the years, one of my favorite theater projects was doing a fundraiser every October called "Haunted Happenings." Theater patrons would stroll through town by the light of a lantern to be entertained with tales of the macabre and supernatural. These were all classic ghost stories spun superbly by period costumed actors.

In June of 2003, I had to have both of my hands operated on for carpal tunnel syndrome, I spent the entire summer recovering and doing rehab to get back the use of my hands. It must be standard advice from all doctors but I was told not to lie around. I was to walk, walk and then walk some more. I was fat enough and sitting around all day wasn't going to help me. You can only prowl the streets of your own neighborhood so many times before boredom sets in. To conquer this, I started walking up and down the main streets of Lebanon. These are the same streets that had seen the likes of Charles Dickens and Abraham Lincoln. Now it was my time.

Being the social animal that I am, I would stop in the shops and visit with the owners. Through doing Haunted Happenings for many years, and appearing on stage at the local theater, many of the shopkeepers knew me and were now friends. Most of them knew my interest in the telling of ghostly tales, but didn't know how serious I was to gather real stories of the paranormal.

By the second week of my treks through Lebanon, one shop owner after another started telling me about the real happenings in their establishments. Over the last several years I have investigated shop after shop and quite frankly, I believe that Lebanon could give any town a run for its money when it comes to being the most haunted small town in the country.

Come with me now for a leisurely midnight stroll through the streets of Lebanon. This is a town where the history of the past intertwines with the present. This is where that tap on the shoulder, that whisper in the ear or those footsteps on the old wooden floor may not have physical bodies attached to them. Along your journey through these pages just remember the famous words of the Godfather of Ghost-Hunting, Harry Price: "We do not know what happens to us when we die, or where we go to, or how we get there. And, if we come back...we do not know how that occurs either. I reiterate that we know nothing about these things, which must have puzzled mankind since the beginning of time. Of course, there are theories, and the most brilliant intellects have for hundreds of years been trying to solve the problems. They have not succeeded!"

WELCOME TO LEBANON

Lebanon is a small mountainous country in the Middle East, north of Israel. Until 15 years of civil war tore it apart, Lebanon was a prosperous country with an economy driven by tourism, banking and agriculture. Oh shoot! Never mind! I had a brain fart. Wrong Lebanon. Okay, let's try this again.

The town of Lebanon, Illinois, is located 22 miles due east of St. Louis, Mo., and around 11 miles northeast of Belleville, the county seat. Governor William Kinney and Thomas Ray first laid out this small community of elegant residences in 1814. The earliest settlers first arrived in 1804. In the spring of 1804, William H. Bradsly and two other young men arrived from Kentucky. These gentlemen choose a location on Silver Creek, around three miles north of present-day Lebanon, where they made improvements to the land and started raising crops. The fall of 1804 saw William's father bring the rest of the family up from Kentucky. In a pioneer history of the area, the Bradsly family were described as brave and energetic folks who were fearless and intrepid, moral and correct.

Being the first settlers must have entitled the Bradslys to naming rights to the town. The Bradslys had come from Lebanon, Kentucky, so naturally, the new community would be called Lebanon.

Now, I should explain the term "first settlers". The Bradslys were by no means the first to inhabit the area. Before 900 A.D., American Indians roamed the prairies of Lebanon and St. Clair County. Their legacy can be seen to this day in the Great Emerald Mound, located northeast of town. This is believed to be a part of the Cahokia mound system. This is not a burial mound, as was thought, but a ceremonial mound. Now owned by the state of Illinois, funds are sorrowfully lacking for archaeological studies.

Spain may have claimed the New World in 1492, but England and France were soon on their heels. The French, through their explorations, soon claimed much of the land up and down the Mississippi River. They failed to gain a large foothold in the Lebanon area. Most likely, this was the result of numerous Indian attacks. The French eventually lost their empire in North America to the British around 1763.

Illinois was originally the Northwest Territory of the Commonwealth of Virginia. In 1780, Virginia delegates deeded this territory to the newly founded United States of America. The Illinois Territory was founded in 1787.

In 1790, General Arthur St. Clair was appointed governor of the Illinois Territory. At the time, General St. Clair was the president of the Continental Congress. He was the one who laid out St. Clair County, in which Lebanon lies, making it the oldest county in Illinois.

Another interesting tidbit about Lebanon was that it was settled by pioneers from Pennsylvania and Ohio. A large German migration, with some English immigrants, filled the area. Also, around 1809, former slaves Austin Lyons, John Titus and John Shaves, who had been freed by Governor Ninian Edwards, the first territorial governor, settled in the Lebanon area.

After the War of 1812, southern Illinois saw settlers from the South migrate up the Mississippi River, move down the Ohio River, then move overland to the West.

In 1816, the United States government granted a parcel of land to Richard Bradsly. Bradsly, in turn, gave the land to trustees of the Lebanon Seminary. This was the beginning of McKendree College.

In 1818, Illinois was admitted to the Union.

1828 saw the actual birth of McKendree College by the Methodists. The name was in honor of Bishop McKendree, who gave 480 acres of land in the Shiloh Valley to the school.

In 1837, according to the Illinois Gazeteer & Business Directory, Lebanon had a steam mill for manufacturing grain and an ox mill for grinding flour; a post office; two public houses (that's taverns, folks); several stores; one grocery; three physicians and about 60 families.

McKendree College was granted university status in 1839. A young man by the name of Abraham Lincoln, then a member of the Illinois General Assembly, helped in this enterprise.

Augustus Chaplin French retired to Lebanon in 1854, after two terms as governor of Illinois. His home, on Belleville Street, was in the Vinegar Hill section of town. The west end of town got this name because all the prohibitionists lived there, while east Lebanon was called Whiskey Flats, for obvious reasons.

1857 saw Lebanon connected with St. Louis, Mo., with the completion of the Baltimore & Ohio Railroad. Goods could now be transported more easily and quickly. Big city influences also made their way into the tiny community.

St. Louis Street in Lebanon when it was still a dirt road

In 1876 black students are integrated in the public school when the school board minutes of July 1876 reported, "The board voted unanimously to place the colored children and grade them in the same rooms with the white children."

The German school for children whose parents wished them to continue speaking that language in their studies, was under the auspices of the Lebanon Public School Board and was taught in one room of the school until the onset of U.S. involvement in World War I.

During the Civil War, 4,400 men from St. Clair County joined the Union side. The McKendree Regiment fought as the 117th.

President Lincoln issued the Emancipation Proclamation on January 1, 1863 freeing all the slaves. The Illinois legislature denounced this as total subversion and a revolution in social organization. So much for practicing what you preach. Up to this time, the residents of Lebanon, black and white, had and still do, a harmonious relationship. People were seen as individuals, not as a color.

Major General James Wilson, a McKendrean, captured Confederate President Jefferson Davis, in 1865.

The Lebanon Public Schools begin in 1872, with one principal, seven teachers and one janitor. An organized school system was needed to cope with the almost 1,500 young people under the age of 21.

Coal was discovered in 1873. It was determined that Lebanon and the

The second block of St. Louis Street in Lebanon, looking east in the 1920s

surrounding area sat atop 50,000 square miles of bituminous coal. In St. Clair County, an astonishing 400,000 acres were underlaid with coal. St. Clair was the largest coal-producing county west of Pennsylvania, with 90 mines and over 3,000 miners. It was also first in the entire state for garden products and second in the production of wheat.

Lebanon became an official city in 1874, with H.H. Horner as its first mayor.

An epidemic of scarlet fever ravaged the town in 1892. The public school was closed while the classrooms were thoroughly fumigated.

During the 1890s, the house at 326 West St. Louis St. became the home of Fred Pesold, a music professor at McKendree. Pesold was a descendant of Johann Sebastian Bach and a friend of the composer Richard Wagner.

During the Spanish-American War, the Commander of the U.S. forces in the Philippines was Major General Wesley Merritt, who grew up in Lebanon and attended McKendree College before graduating from West Point.

The young folks should love this: In 1899, the high school course of study lasted two years. The class salutatorian was 15-year-old Benjamin Howard McAllister.

1899 also brought the tiny town a reputation as a resort area and cultural

A streetcar traveling west on St. Louis Street

mecca. With hotels, bands, McKendree College and the Illinois Literary and Commercial Institute and School of Art, trips outside the area to broaden the mind weren't required.

An interurban railway was built between St. Louis and Lebanon in 1903. City dwellers could more easily escape the summer heat and enjoy some of Lebanon's other delights. These included mineral water bottled by the Lebanon Soda and Mineral Water Factory. Chautauqua Week and a summer songfest known as the Sangverein attracted tourists from all around.

Al Steidel won a bowling tournament in Lebanon in 1904. Big deal, huh? Well, it was. First prize was an all-expense-paid trip to the World's Fair in St. Louis. The value of the prize came to about $4.68, which included 75 cents round trip fare on the new electric railway. Top that, Deal or no Deal!

In the great state of Illinois, in 1905, both the governor and lieutenant governor were McKendree graduates. Also, two congressmen, three college presidents, and two judges on the state Supreme Court graduated from this prestigious institution.

In 1911, Charles Dickens' son, Francis, visited Lebanon. I did not mention the elder Dickens' visit in 1842 because he will be a significant player in a later tale.

In 1917 fire destroyed some of the largest businesses in town. The city's fire engine, a hand pumper, wouldn't work. This fiasco led to the creation of The Lebanon Volunteer Fire Department, which to this day, can match up against the best.

The Spanish Influenza (a virulent strain of the flu) spread like wildfire across the United States in 1918. This epidemic ravaged St. Clair County, killing hundreds.

Yearly debates over the use of alcohol also raged at this time. The town was so divided over the issue that two areas grew up: Vinegar Hill and Whiskey Flats."

The federal government purchased the land for Scott Air Base was in 1919 for $119,285.

A new high school building was dedicated in 1922. The (for the time) enormous class of 41 students created a teacher shortage.

In 1928, Charles Lindberg landed his monoplane at Scott Field rather than St. Louis because the runway lighting was better.

McKendree College celebrated its centennial in 1928, graduating 58 students, its largest class ever.

The Great Depression of the 1930s brought serious unemployment to Lebanon. The Grauel barbershop reduced the price of haircuts to 25 cents.

The school board in 1938 was devastated to learn that a teacher helped students prepare banners for a demonstration.

After World War II, the entire country enjoyed a construction boom. Lebanon was no exception. The ranch-style house became the rage and Lebanon saw its share of these popular single-story homes.

Corner of North Pearl and West St. Louis Street in Lebanon in 1906. L. Traband moved his general merchandise store to this location after the Heer family bought his property across the street. It is now home to the Cross-Eyed Elephant.

In 1950, Doc Freshour, a local druggist, reported the largest sale of aspirin in the town's history. His explanation was, "London had its Black Plague, Ireland had its potato famine and McKendree College had its final exams!"

Tragedy struck on April 30, 1950, when a B-25 from Scott Air Force Base crashed in Lebanon only 15 minutes after takeoff. All six crewmen were killed. The only recognizable piece of the plane that was salvaged after the crash was a wheel. The plane was only 200 yards short of the open field that its pilot was desperately trying to reach. Though numerous small injuries occurred, no civilians lost their lives due to the valiant efforts of the airmen.

Also in 1950, Lebanon's population had grown to over 2,400.

The 1960s brought an improvement that could have proven devastating to the tiny community. The interstate highway system diverted much-needed traffic from the town and moved it to the larger shopping centers. Rather than view this as a negative, Lebanon embraced this setback as a way to hold onto its best asset, a rich architectural heritage.

A 1961 excavation of the Emerald Mound uncovered a fire pit dating back to about 1300 A. D.

The Lebanon Historical Society was quickly formed in 1964 to purchase the Mermaid Inn (you will hear more about this building in a later chapter). Leon Church was the society's first president.

The Emerald Mound was purchased and preserved in 1968 by Col. Henry Crown, a Chicago philanthropist.

In 1970, a national census placed Mascoutah, eight miles south of Lebanon, as the U.S. center of population. In 170 years, Lebanon had moved from the nation's western boundary to its center.

The Lebanon of today looks very much like the town of yesteryear. Homes of Gothic, Italianate, English Country, Queen Anne, Georgian and Southern Colonial style are everywhere. The downtown buildings date from the 1850s to the 1870s.

Perhaps Lebanon's major tourist attraction was the Looking Glass Prairie. From the mid-1810s to around 1870, it was common to name prairies. Names were usually based upon animals or plants that were native to the area, or by whatever inspired the persons gazing upon them at the time. Legend has it that Looking Glass Prairie was so named because when in bloom, it appeared to be as smooth as glass.

I know this is a small timeline for so much history. One might call it the "Reader's Digest condensed version", but I don't want to bog the reader down with a historical term paper.

As we move from story to story on our journey, historical tidbits from each location will be revealed to fill in the blanks. So, follow me on a historical, hair-raising journey and remember: Man always fears what he does not understand!

A TIME TO SAY GOODBYE

One of the shopkeepers whom I met on my travels through Lebanon was Michele Rowe. Michele is the owner of the Town N' Country Shop. This antique, collectable and gift shop has been operated by the Rowe family since 1975. A mutual friend had alerted me to a possible ghost story connected with Michele.

In June 2005, during one of my rehab strolls through town (this time for my back), I happened into Town N' Country looking for a candle. Michele was by herself, no customers in the shop. This was a change because the place is usually packed with shoppers. As a conversation with me always does, our little chat soon turned to talk of ghosts and hauntings. Michele said she had wanted to talk to me about a possible haunting, but wasn't sure how to approach me. Now, with no one else around, the time was right. Michele started to tell me about the house where she had grown up, along with her brother, Ed.

Michele's parents, Charles and Althea Rowe, had bought the house in 1963. The two-story brick structure, built in the federal style, was erected around 1847. The longest ownership of the house was by Joseph James McKee and his wife, Lillie, from 1867 to 1920. This was the first home in Lebanon to be presented with a landmark plaque for architectural value by the St. Clair County Historical Society.

Michele informed me that the house was going up for sale in four days and she wanted to know if I would take a look at it. She wouldn't say that it was haunted, only that there were strong sensations in the house.

Later that day, I met Michele at her childhood home. It had certainly seen better days. Five years of sitting empty after a major fire, had done considerable damage to the place. I could see the pain and nostalgia in Michele's eyes as we made our way through the rooms. This was a place she loved, but could no longer afford to keep.

In December 2000, Althea was living alone in the house. Charles had passed away several years before. A strong-willed woman of 71, Althea didn't entertain guests so much as hold court. Seated in her chair by the fireplace in the sitting room, she was a commanding presence.

The house where Michelle's mother died in a tragic fire

We all have our little vices and Althea had two of them. To say she smoked would be misleading. Althea would light up a cigarette, take a puff, and then let it almost burn itself out before taking one last drag. She also liked to have a cocktail or two, during the day, but never to excess.

That December, Althea was battling several ailments that caused her to become dizzy. These spells usually didn't last long and would be soon forgotten. No one knows for sure if the dizzy spells, the smoking or the cocktails caused the fire that day. It didn't matter because the result was the same: Althea perished in a fire in the summer kitchen.

Over the next five years, Michele would battle with insurance companies, contractors, and even her brother, Ed, over what to do with the house. It sustained a heavy amount of smoke and fire damage. The contractors that the insurance companies insisted on using caused more damage. By the time I saw the house it was a wreck. The wallpaper was stained and torn. Large pieces of plaster had fallen from the ceilings and walls. The summer kitchen had been torn down and rebuilt by people I wouldn't hire to build a tree house. This once-proud structure now sat silent and forlorn. Michele's brother was pressing her to sell the place. She finally gave in and the house and property would shortly be going on the auction block.

Memories overwhelmed Michele as we went from room to room. After about an hour, she had to go back to the store. I decided to stay awhile longer.

I always say that you should trust your gut in any situation. That extra little voice has helped me many times. As I walked Michele outside, she said that she always had the feeling that her mother had passed out due to a dizzy spell, and hit her head on the island in the kitchen. After the fire, it was discovered that Althea's head had sustained a hard blow from something.

Paranormal investigating had always been fun for me but his was the first time that I had a friend involved. The sadness in her eyes didn't make this easy.

When Michele left, I went back inside. After wandering through the house, I decided to concentrate my efforts in the sitting room and the kitchen.

Michele never claimed that the house was haunted. I think she just wanted to know if any remnants of her family still existed there. Because she was a friend, I said I'd check and see what I could find. Nothing out of the ordinary came up on the TriField Meter. I snapped several photos. Nothing but the dust that I had stirred up appeared on them. The entire time I walked through the house I had been asking questions out loud and was hoping to record answers on my tape recorder. On entering the sitting room, I decided to put the tape recorder on the fireplace mantle and just sit and ask questions.

To my amazement, the recorder came on! It kept stopping and starting on its own. After about ten minutes, the tape ran out. I decided that this was enough for one day, so I picked up my toys and went out to the car.

The excitement was too much for me. Instead of listening to the tape when I got home, as I had planned, I rewound it in the driveway. All the answers, which were surely on the tape, might provide Michele with some closure and I would have proof of the existence of the other side. Instead, my amazement turned to amusement as nothing but my voice popped up on the tape. On examining the tape recorder, I found that when I placed it on the fireplace mantle, I had accidentally switched it to the voice activate mode. I had been recording myself the entire time!

Not to be deterred, I went back to the house the next day with Bill Alsing, the owner of the History & Hauntings Bookstore in Alton. Bill and I made our way through the entire house and came up with nothing unusual. After relating my adventure with the tape recorder, we decided to try it again. This time we would carefully check all the buttons. I placed the tape recorder and Bill's TriField Meter on the fireplace mantle. At the doorway between the sitting room and the kitchen, we set my TriField Meter. We then asked that if anyone was present with us, to give us a sign such as a rap on the wall or something physical that we could see or hear. When nothing happened, we decided to walk around the outside of the house. I've found that sometimes the entities are bashful and don't like an audience.

The TriField Meters that Bill and I use are electronic devices that measure levels and changes in magnetic fields. They have been adapted for use by paranormal researchers with the idea that the presence of a ghost, or paranormal activity of any kind, may affect the atmosphere of a location. The TriField Meter, made by AlphaLabs, is one of the more sensitive devices available. It makes it easy to rule out magnetic changes caused by electric wiring and other artificial sources.

As Bill and I got back to the summer kitchen, Michele pulled up in the driveway. She was getting ready to leave on a well-deserved vacation and she wanted to know if we had found anything. The heartache and demands of the past five years, coupled with a bad head cold and frazzled nerves, were taking its toll on her. Michele just needed to get out of town before the house auction. She needed to get away and bring an end to a sorrowful chapter of her life.

With tears in her eyes, Michele entered the new summer kitchen area with us and then followed us into the kitchen. As we stood there, both of our TriField Meters went crazy. The tape recorder was working on its own and it wasn't on the voice-activated mode. This went on for 30 minutes. As much as she wanted to stay, Michele had to leave. Her vacation destination was calling. As I walked her out to the car, I promised to let her know what we found when she returned.

As I went back into the sitting room, I saw Bill standing there wide-eyed. He said that as soon as Michele and I went outside, everything stopped. On examining the tape recorder, we found nothing on the tape. The TriField Meters were silent. We made one last sweep of the house and did pick up a few readings on the meters in an upstairs bedroom, but that was all.

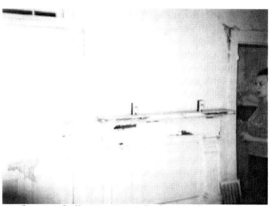

When Michelle came into the house, the meters on the fireplace began going off with no explanation

As we discussed this case amongst ourselves, and with a few American Ghost Society members who were more qualified than we were, we all came to the same conclusion: we believe that the house held many memories for Michele. They were all good until the last five years. Then this place of happiness and joy had turned into a nightmare for her. Her mother's death and the fighting with insurance companies and family members had worn her down. She just wanted closure.

Because the last time Michele entered the house would be the final time, I feel that she was overwhelmed with emotions. These emotions, coupled with her cold and the need to say goodbye, may have caused the equipment to go crazy. I've always felt that nothing is stronger than human emotions. I honestly believe that Michele's emotional energy made the equipment come to life. When she left the house, everything stopped.

The house has since been sold and the new owners are putting some much-needed work into the place. The best part of the investigation for me was being able to help a friend. By finding nothing unusual in the house, we were able to help Michele cope with her grief and bring an end to a painful chapter of her life.

As of this writing, Michele is putting the family business up for sale. Actually, the location will eventually be sold. She will still do shows for her products and possibly sell merchandise online. I know things change but it's always a bit sad when a friend moves away. I wish Michele peace and happiness in her new surroundings.

HELLO, IS ANYBODY THERE?

It would have been easy to title this chapter "All That Jazz" because the current business at 230 W. Saint Louis St. is called the Dr. Jazz Soda Fountain and Grill. That would be too easy! Instead you get the title you've just read. Now that the pain medicine for my bad back has kicked in we can get to the actual story.

It was a dark and stormy night, no, wait a minute! It was a bright and sunny day in 2000, when I met Paul Krumsieg. Paul, with the help of his family and associates, has restored the two-story brick building at the corner of St. Clair and West St. Louis streets to its original grandeur. I had noticed the building sitting empty for several years and had hoped that someone would come and breathe some life back into the old place. From the ashes, you might say, arose Dr. Jazz.

Today, when you step through the door, you literally, step back in time. It's a time of '40s and '50s jazz and the good old soda fountain. The girls behind the counter never fail to greet you with a smile and they genuinely want to know how you're doing. As good as the food is, it doesn't stop you from rushing through your meal to get to the dessert. My favorite is the "Maple Leaf Rag." This mountainous bowl of maple-flavored ice cream with all the fixings is definitely generous enough for two people.

Wait! Wasn't I supposed to be writing about ghosts? Oh well, cold things are cold things. Let's just say that Dr. Jazz is holding its own in these tough economic times.

Now, Paul is a good, God-fearing man with whom I've become friends anyway. He knew of my interest in the paranormal and told me he didn't necessarily believe in that stuff himself. I did get Paul to promise me that if anything happened at Dr. Jazz that he couldn't explain, he would call me.

Within a couple of months, I got the call. Paul had bought the place from William Freshour. The Freshour family had owned the property since 1915, when Orville Freshour bought the former Lebanon Drug Company. William was Orville's son and he operated the

Dr. Jazz Soda Fountain & Grill

business until he retired in 1996. It was   called, appropriately enough, Freshour's Drug Store. Not only did the store sell drugs, but you could also purchase candy, stationery supplies and even house paint there.

William Freshour passed away not too long ago but not without first relating an interesting tale to Paul. Paul, in turn, passed the following story on to me.

There is a phone booth in the back of the ice cream parlor that was built on December 7, 1941, the day Pearl Harbor was bombed. No, the phone booth is not haunted by the Japanese! Freshour told Paul that in 1990, the phone booth had been moved to the middle of the floor during some renovation when the phone began to ring as if someone were making a call. There's nothing strange about that, right? But the phone booth was not connected to a power source. In fact, it hadn't been hooked up and working for almost 30 years! At first, Freshour tried to ignore the ringing but eventually curiosity got the better of him. He sat down in the booth and put the receiver to his ear. No voice greeted him. There was only a small burst of static followed by dead silence. After that, the mysterious caller, whoever it was, became quite persistent. The phone just kept ringing. Finally, silence reigned when Freshour cut the bells for the ringer off. Today, the phone resides in its original place of honor. As far as we know, no calls have been received.

This strange tale (and you know I'm into the strange stuff) piqued my interest. So, what was I to do but dig into the history of the site? I found out that the store at 230 W. Saint Louis St. was built in 1850. It was originally a pharmacy.

The 1940s telephone booth at Dr. Jazz where mysterious calls from beyond have been received.

According to the Illinois State Gazetteer & Business Directory for 1890-1891, a T.A. Wilson was listed as the owner. Wilson ran a pharmacy called the Lebanon Drug Company. Now, we know how a tragedy, especially an untimely death, can cause a haunting. Sadly, this location had such an occurrence. A man named L.L. Pfeffer leased the building from 1891 through 1914. He continued to run the business as the Lebanon Drug Company. Not only was this a pharmacy, but the shop also had a soda fountain. The soda fountain was installed in 1887 and is still operational to this day. From what I've been told, it is one of only two of its kind in North America.

L.L. Pfeffers' 23-year-old son, Robert, was the manager of the store. A McKendree graduate who excelled in athletics, Robert Pfeffer was a familiar sight riding his motorcycle around town. One dark and stormy day in 1912, he was at the soda fountain preparing a soft drink when he was electrocuted by a lightening strike to the building. This was in the days before ground fault interrupters. At the time of the accident, the soda fountain was located in the front right section of the store, just inside the front door.

After Robert's untimely death, The Freshour family took over the business. During the Freshour proprietorship the soda fountain was moved to its current location in the back left section of the store.

The building not only housed the drugstore. From 1895 until 1908, Dr. Edward C. Hammond ran a dental office upstairs. Hammond moved to Lebanon from Jefferson City, Mo., to start his practice.

Until 1943, the upstairs front section of the building housed the switchboard for the local telephone company. In 1906, the Smiley Telephone Company was born in Lebanon. When Bell Telephone bought the company in 1947, it was providing service to 397 customers. The exchange was then moved to West Center Street. The Lebanon telephone office was closed in 1952 when Bell moved its operations to

O'Fallon.

When Paul Krumsieg first took over the building, he told me about hearing strange noises from upstairs. He said it often sounded like footsteps. Of course with a structure of its age, the footsteps can be explained away as old plumbing and the building settling. Paul has since renovated the entire second floor and turned it into a bed and breakfast. Today's footsteps now have bodies attached to them.

Even though the soda fountain has been moved, an occasional cold spot can be experienced in the front right section of the store, where it was located when young Robert Pfeffer met his tragic end.

The newest ghostly twist has come from the staff. The computer where the waitresses type in their orders sits off the soda fountain in the rear of the store, next to the old phone booth. New employees have been experiencing taps on their shoulders, as well as the feeling of fingers running through their hair. More often than not, these happenings occur at the end of the day when the waitresses are getting ready to close up.

So whether you enjoy your cold spots in a phone booth, at a soda fountain, or in a huge schooner, Dr. Jazz should be music for your tastes, otherworldly or not.

The antique soda and ice cream fountain at Dr. Jazz

THE MERMAID HOUSE INN

Sitting peacefully along the first block of East Main Street is a small two-story structure that pre-dates most of the other buildings in Lebanon. The Mermaid House Inn was built in 1830 by retired sea Captain Lyman Adams.

Captain Adams was born in Hartford, Conn., in February 1779. At the ripe old age of 11, Adams left his home to become a sailor. After many years at sea, he finally became captain of his own ship. The merchant sea trade was his calling. Eventually giving up the bounding main for a life on terra firma, he settled in Baltimore where became a recorder in the police court.

Adams was a militia commander during the War of 1812, in defense of the city of Baltimore. He fought the British at the Battle of Blodensburg.

After the war, Adams went to Louisville, Ky., where he was employed in the merchandising   business. In 1829, he left Louisville and settled in Lebanon. He built the Mermaid House Inn in 1830. It was a combination inn and dry goods store.

Adams named his new establishment The Mermaid House Inn because he actually believed that while at sea those many years, he really did see mermaids. Now, you must remember that in those days, fresh water didn't last long at sea. A variety of liquids that wouldn't go bad on the open ocean were used on all ships. These included grog, rum, beer, etc. I'm sure that these refreshments would cause many of us to see mermaids.

This inn could never be confused with today's Hilton hotels. It was more like a Motel 6. Although it wasn't fancy, it was a very busy place as travel through Lebanon was quite heavy in those days. The town of Lebanon was situated on the main stage line between Cincinnati and St. Louis. This route, today's old Highway

50, was know as the Vincennes Trail.

The more stylish Bishop House was located across the alley, facing the public square.

On April 12, 1842, author Charles Dickens and his traveling party came to Lebanon from St. Louis to see the Looking Glass Prairie. Captain Adams owned the land east of Lebanon from which the Dickens party viewed the prairie. This connection is probably what led Dickens to stay at the Mermaid House.

During the frontier days of Illinois, from about 1818 to 1870, it was a common practice to name the local prairies much the same way as the towns and cities were named. Many colorful names arose, such as Froggy Prairie;

The Mermaid House

Macoupin Prairie; Crow; Horse, and Bull's Eye prairies. The Looking Glass Prairie is now located in St. Clair and Madison counties.

Englishman William Oliver traveled through southern and central Illinois in 1841. He wrote the following description of the Looking Glass Prairie: 'A few miles farther on we entered on a branch of Looking Glass Prairie, Bond County, where long reaches of green undulating prairie stretched away until they became lost in the haze of distance and, within a few hours of sunset, we emerged from a grove and the prairie lay stretched out before us like an ocean. In the direction which the track we were following took, we could just distinguish the forest like a low bank of clouds, whilst on our right the prairie stretched away, one vast plain, uninterrupted by tree or bush, as far as the eye could reach.'

Dickens and his traveling party consisted of 14 members, plus two stagecoach drivers. At the time of his visit, the Mermaid House was much larger than it is today and had outbuildings to house large parties. Adams owned much of the block, as well as a farm about two miles east of the inn.

In Dickens book, "American Notes," published in 1846, not many good things were printed about the area. Lebanon could easily have felt the author's wrath. Due to a late winter, the Looking Glass Prairie wasn't in full bloom when Dickens arrived. That, coupled with a disappointing trip through Belleville put Dickens in a sour mood. Captain Lyman Adams and his family soon changed Dickens outlook. Here are the author's own words:

From Belleville, we went on, through the same desolate kind of waste, and constantly attended, without the interval of a moment, by the same music; until, at three o'clock in the afternoon, we halted once more at a village called Lebanon to inflate the horses again, and give them some corn besides, of which they stood much in need. Pending this ceremony, I walked into the village, where I met a full-sized dwelling-house coming downhill at a round trot, drawn by a score or more of oxen.

The public house was so very clean and good a one, that the managers of the jaunt resolved to return to it and put up there for the night, if possible. This course decided on, and the horses being well refreshed, we again pushed forward, and came upon the Prairie at sunset.

It would be difficult to say why, or how - though it was possibly from having heard and read so much about it - but the effect on me was disappointment. Looking towards the setting sun, there lay, stretched out before my view, a vast expanse of level ground; unbroken, save by one thin line of trees, which scarcely amounted to a scratch upon the great blank; until it met the glowing sky, wherein it seemed to dip: mingling with its rich colours, and mellowing in its distant blue. There it lay, a tranquil sea or lake without water, if such a simile be admissible, with the day going down upon it: a few birds wheeling here and there: and solitude and silence reigning paramount around. But the grass was not yet high; there were bare black patches on the ground; and the few wild flowers that the eye could see, were poor and scanty. Great as the picture was, its very flatness and extent, which left nothing to the imagination, tamed it down and cramped its interest. I felt little of that sense of freedom and exhilaration which a Scottish heath inspires, or even our English downs awaken. It was lonely and wild, but oppressive in its barren monotony. I felt that in traversing the Prairies, I could never abandon myself to the scene, forgetful of all else; as I should do instinctively, were there heather underneath my feet, or an ironbound coast beyond; but should often glance towards the distant and frequently receding line of the horizon, and wish it gained and passed. It is not a scene to be forgotten, but it is scarcely one, I think (at all events, as I saw it), to remember with much pleasure, or to covet the looking-on again, in after-life.

We encamped near a solitary log-house, for the sake of its water, and dined upon the plain. The baskets contained roast fowls, buffalo's tongue (an exquisite dainty, by the way), ham, bread, cheese, and butter; biscuits, champagne, sherry; lemons and sugar for punch; and abundance of rough ice. The meal was delicious, and the entertainers were the soul of kindness and good humour. I have often recalled that cheerful party to my pleasant recollection since, and shall not easily forget, in junketings nearer home with friends of older date, my boon companions on the Prairie.

Returning to Lebanon that night, we lay at the little inn at which we had halted in the afternoon. In point of cleanliness and comfort it would have suffered by no comparison with any

English alehouse, of homely kind, in England.

Rising at five o'clock next morning, I took a walk about the village: none of the houses were strolling about to-day, but it was early for them yet, perhaps: and then amused myself by lounging in a kind of farm-yard behind the tavern, of which the leading features were a strange jumble of rough sheds for stables; a rude colonnade, built as a cool place of summer resort; a deep well; a great earthen mound for keeping vegetables in, in winter time; and a pigeon-house, whose little apertures looked, as they do in all pigeon-houses, very much too small for the admission of the plump and swelling-breasted birds who were strutting about it, thought they tried to get in never so hard. That interest exhausted, I took a survey of the inn's two parlours, which were decorated with coloured prints of Washington, and President Madison, and of a white-faced young lady (Much speckled by the flies), who held up her gold neck-chain for the admiration of the spectator, and informed all admiring comers that she was "Just Seventeen" although I should have thought her older. In the best room were two oil portraits of the kit-cat size, representing the landlord and his infant son; both looking as bold as lions, and staring out of the canvas with an intensity that would have been cheap at any price. They were painted, I think by the artist who had touched up the Belleville doors with red and gold; for I seemed to recognize his style immediately.

After breakfast, we started to return by a different way from that which we had taken yesterday, and coming up at ten o'clock with an encampment of German emigrants carrying their goods in carts, who had made a rousing fire which they were just quitting, stopped there to refresh. And very pleasant the fire was; for, hot though it had been yesterday, it was quite cold to-day, and the wind blew keenly. Looming in the distance, as we rode along, was another of the ancient Indian burial-places, called The Monks' Mound in memory of a body of fanatics of the order of La Trappe, who founded a desolate convent there, many years ago, when there were no settlers within a thousand miles, and were all swept off by the pernicious climate in which lamentable fatality, few rational people will suppose, perhaps, that society experienced any very severe deprivation.'

The preceding observations are from Dickens' book, "American Notes," about his trip to the United States. Lucky chapter 13 was entitled, "A Jaunt to the Looking Glass Prairie and Back."

Besides playing host to the famous author and his party, Adams was also very well acquainted with many of the prominent state politicians of the day, especially those of the Democratic party, of which he was an active and strong supporter.

Innkeeper was not his only the moniker, as for many years he served as Lebanon's postmaster, justice of the peace and Notary Public. His good business habits made him popular, not only locally but also throughout the county. Adams had 11 children by his last wife, whose mother was a Lebanon native. Adams went to meet his maker on July 2, 1851.

Now everyone and his brother seem to have an Abraham Lincoln story, especially in Illinois. Lebanon and the Mermaid House Inn are no exception. According to descendants of Lyman Adams, a stagecoach bearing Lincoln and some other passengers stopped at the Mermaid House Inn for a much-needed meal. Lincoln was a notoriously slow eater and was only halfway through his meal when the others left the inn without him. Lincoln brought it to Captain Adams' attention that there was no silver at the place settings and that someone from the coach must have made off with the utensils. Adams, being the inn's proprietor as well as the local law official, took off to stop the coach. He caught up to it just west of town at the whisky distillery and brought it back to the Mermaid House. Lincoln, now finished with his meal, informed Adams that he had found the silverware in the coffee pot. The story, though unverifiable, is charming enough to be told over and over.

Adams sold the property in 1845. The new owner subdivided it into individual lots, which he then sold, causing the original building to be partially sliced. The house that you see today is what is left from that butchering. The rear two rooms were added at this time, thus placing an exterior window in an interior wall, and a back room divider that is reminiscent of porch construction.

In 1905 the property was purchased by Frederick "Fritz" Caupe as a wedding present to his son and daughter-in-law, Henry and Emma Caupe. The house stayed in the Caupe family until November 4, 1964, when it was purchased by the Lebanon Historical Society, which was founded by Leon H. Church for the purpose of acquiring the historic building. Restoration efforts were put on hold, as Church's full attention was needed to help save the Emerald Mound, which was being sold for fill.

The mound was erected by the Mississippian culture of mound-building Indians around 900-1000 A.D. It is located one and one-half miles northeast of Lebanon. Due to Church's efforts, the Emerald Mound is now owned by the state of Illinois and is administered by the state Department of Conservation in Springfield.

By 1973, the historical society began work on restoring the Mermaid House. Private and public donations, along with 10 years of Miss Mermaid contests have financed the work. Restoration has been done so as to leave visible sections of the original features. These include hand-hewn oak beams held together by wooden pegs

The headstone of Captain Lyman Adams

and the original plaster (mixed with horse hair for added strength), applied over hand- cut laths. The original fireplace and chimneys have been replaced, as they were deemed too weak to be repaired. The floors are mostly original except for those sections that had to be removed to allow installation of new support beams in the cellar. The Mermaid House Inn was added to the National Register of Historic Places on December 14, 1975.

Charles Dickens returned to the United States shortly before his death in 1870 but he did not make it back to Lebanon. His son, Francis, came here just after the turn of the 20th century, and his great-grandson, Cedric Charles Dickens, came to the inn for a reception in January of 1986.

My personal involvement with the Mermaid House Inn started about 1999. The Looking Glass Playhouse needed a place to hold its annual fundraiser, Haunted Happenings, and the Lebanon Historical Society graciously allowed the use of the inn. The inn actually provided two story-telling locations: one was in the rear of the building next to Captain Adams' headstone and the other was inside, next to the fireplace in the front room. Yes, I did say Captain Adams' headstone! Someone in the historical society found out that Captain Adams' descendants had gotten a new headstone for the old boy and put it at his gravesite in the local cemetery. The historical society was able to obtain the old headstone and put it in a place of honor in the garden of the Mermaid House. The only time there is a body there is during the telling of classic horror stories every October.

The indoor location for the story telling has proven to be far more fruitful pertaining to real ghosts. These happenings were related to me by two of my friends from the Looking Glass Theater. They knew of my interest in the paranormal, but were hesitant at first to relate what happened to them for hear of ridicule, and because they just didn't believe in ghosts. These ladies had, and still have, no knowledge of each other's story. I was asked, for obvious reasons, not to use their real names.

The doorway in the Mermaid House where the strange figures were seen during the Haunted Happenings events.

As I stated earlier, the indoor Haunted happenings stories at the Mermaid House were told next to the fireplace in the front room. The storyteller would be seated in a rocking chair with a small fire in the fireplace. A costumed actor would lead the patrons into the front room and seat them on the floor. When everyone was seated and all was quiet the tale would begin. Those of us who work these events, as well as those of us who conduct tours, watch where everyone goes as they enter our location. We don't need anybody jumping out of the darkness to try and give us a fright. Yes, there is always one knucklehead in the group. We want full control of the area. Also, during storytelling of my kind, eye contact is essential.

Now Sue had the storytelling duties on Friday and Emmy had them on Saturday. Within five days after the event, both ladies had approached me. Each had no knowledge of the other but their stories were almost identical. Because Haunted Happenings takes place during mid-October, it is always dark outside for the 6 p.m. start of the tours. The first and second groups through the inn were well behaved and very attentive. Sue's story went without a hitch. As the third group of the night entered the front room, the entire area seemed to have a bit of electricity in it. Sue started her story after scanning the room and making sure that all was as it should be. During her tale, she made eye contact with the guests, moving from right to left. At the end of the row of patrons on the left was a doorway that led to the other front room. The doorway had been empty while the tour guide was standing next to Sue. On her third pass over the seated guests something in the doorway caught her eye. Standing there were three people in turn-of-the-century clothing. They were two men and a woman and they appeared to be listening to Sue's story with interest.

The adage that insists the show must go on applied even here. Sue swept her gaze to the right then back to the left. Thankfully, the three figures standing in the shadows were gone. As soon as the story was over, Sue asked the guide if he had brought any extra people into the building. The guide assured her that he had not. A quick inspection after everyone had left revealed that Sue was indeed alone in the house. Fortunately, the next group was arriving and the incident would be forgotten. With everyone in place Sue began her talk. This time, on her first sweep of the crowd, the three extra guests were again watching from the doorway. This time they hung around for about a minute, which, of course, seemed like an hour to Sue. When the story was over and the guests had made their way outside, Sue had the tour guide walk through the house with her. Again, there was nothing out of the ordinary. Thankfully for Sue, the rest of the night was uneventful!

Saturday night brought only one change to the tour. Emmy was now doing the storytelling at the Mermaid House. This had nothing to do with Sue's experience. Real life often gets in the way of our pretend world at the theater and Sue had family obligations that night. Fortunately, the Looking Glass Playhouse had a variety of talent to choose from, so Emmy could fill in without missing a beat.

Emmy, unlike Sue, couldn't wait to relate her experiences of the evening. When her stories were done for the night she tracked me down at the theater. Emmy told me how she scanned the crowd during her story as all good weavers of tales do. Twice during the night's entertainment the three extra tour guests were at their station in the doorway. Emmy described them exactly as Sue would in a couple of days. Neither of them believed in ghosts. Something happened that night that both women just couldn't explain.

I am currently the vice-president of the Lebanon Historical Society, which means I went to the bathroom at the wrong time. On my return from nature's call, I discovered I had become an officer. This turned out to be a fortunate turn of events. Because of my office I was able to make the Mermaid House Inn a regular stop on The Haunted Lebanon Tours. For years I had been telling Troy Taylor that I would match Lebanon against any other town, ghost for ghost. He finally told me to put up or shut up. Thus we began the Haunted Lebanon Tours. I'm in the Mermaid House Inn quite frequently. During the Haunted Lebanon Tours our guests have reported cold spots, footsteps and a feeling of being watched. Several patrons have seen a man walking upstairs carrying a lighted candle. Now, almost all of the windows in the building are original, which means they're not perfectly smooth, but very close. I've tested with flashlights and car lights and cannot recreate the things that others have reported seeing.

The inn has some air conditioning in the lower level. This is only turned on for meetings and special events. The tours are not special events, which means, it's sometimes very toasty during a tour.

In the summer of 2007, when the Haunted Lebanon tours were in their infancy, the building was quite stuffy. On one particular Friday night in July, I led my sweaty group of tourists down the back steps and past the makeshift kitchen area. My cabooses for the night were my wife, Kim, my daughter, Megan, and my friend, Zach. (Cabooses follow behind the tour to watch for stragglers and make sure everyone is following the guide.) As Megan passed through the small kitchen area, she stopped

The kitchen area at the Mermaid House. This was formerly the back porch. A chair was moved by unseen hands during a Haunted Lebanon Tour and an icy cold cylinder of air has been experienced on numerous occasions over the table.

to reset a small chair at the table in the middle of the room. Kim and Zach waited for Megan to finish her house cleaning, then all three of them walked past the table and stood in the doorway of the next room where I was entertaining the troops. Kim's spider-sense started to tingle. She turned around and gasped as the chair that Megan had pushed under the table was now several feet away from the table. Megan and Zach also turned around and witnessed the change. What amazed all three of them was that not a sound was heard. The chair had moved in the space of about five seconds. Kim and Megan are both members of my little investigative team, PRIME, which stands for Paranormal Researchers in the Metro-East. Zach is an American Ghost Society member. If they told me it happened, I believe them. None of them would misrepresent the facts.

A couple of nights later, my son, whom I'll call Josh, because that's his name, had some friends fly in from California. It was about 9 p.m. when they arrived at our house. Not being tired and not knowing what to do, I suggested a quick ghost tour of Lebanon. On arriving at the Mermaid House we found the same hot and stuffy rooms greeting us. As we descended the back staircase and reached the kitchen area there was a funnel of freezing cold air surrounding the table from ceiling to floor. When we stuck our arms in the cold spot the hairs stood up and goose bumps popped up. This lasted for five minutes with no reason for it to be happening, as far as we could tell. We went to the next room for a moment and on our return, the funnel of icy air was gone.

I've often told our tour patrons that the scariest part of each tour is when we exit a location. Everyone goes outside but me. I have to go back through and turn out the lights and make sure that all is as it should be. The Mermaid House, although nothing bad is in there, unnerves me a bit at the end of each tour. Whispers, footsteps and cold spots are not at all uncommon. An occasional door even moves.

The Mermaid House is open by appointment and on special occasions. Private groups can use it for meetings. There is no charge for this but donations are happily accepted.

Just remember, when doing a head count, don't be surprised to find a few extra in your party.

TAP ONCE
FOR YES

There are some of you out there who feel that it must be a breeze to write about the things that go bump in the night. If it were a cold, dark, wintry evening you would probably be correct. This warm, summer afternoon finds the sun shining, the birds whistling, and the butterflies doing whatever the hell butterflies do with themselves. Even though all is right with the world around me, I'll try to relocate this tale of the paranormal from my mind to the printed page.

I find no greater joy than investigating paranormal incidents in an active restaurant. By active, I mean a working restaurant serving real food. My day trips to Lebanon brought me to such a place on a regular basis. The Tapestry Room restaurant at 123 W. Saint Louis St. is one of my favorite hangouts. Not only is the food and service exceptional, but also the place is actually haunted.

Prior to the year 2000, I had heard rumors from some of the locals that strange, unexplainable things were going on at the Tapestry Room. The summer of 2003 gave me time to actually follow up on the reports.

Over many lunch trips to the restaurant, I became friends with Pat Peterson, co-manager of the Tapestry Room, which is owned by his sister and brother-in-law, Gwen and Bob Barcum. The restaurant had been operating for years before I showed up. I was just the first one goofy enough to inquire about the possibility of ghosts. As it usually happens, it took a while for Pat to believe that I was serious about the location's ghost stories. Once he saw that I was serious; he had quite a tale to tell.

Years ago, when Pat was readying the restaurant for opening day, he had all

Tapestry Room Restaurant

his ducks in a row except for one. Some wiring still needed to be done to activate the security system. The electricians were supposed to arrive early in the afternoon. At the top of the hour -- that's each and every hour -- the phone calls started to come. The electricians explained that they were running late, but would arrive as soon as possible. As soon as possible turned into 9 p.m. As you can imagine, Pat was furious by the time they finally showed up. Sensing this, one electrician went straight to the basement while the other tried to calm Pat down.

I only bring up this next point because it may have had something to do with what happened next. One of the electricians was white and the other was black. The black electrician was the one who started the job in the basement. The white electrician was getting an earful of complaints from Pat regarding the delay when a sudden shriek of terror rang out from the basement. In a flash, the electrician came running upstairs and right out the front door. During the entire duration of his sprint, the   electrician was screaming about a ghost in the basement. Now, not only was there a mystery afoot, but now the job couldn't be completed because it required two men. Pat, at this point, was more mystified than mad. The evening came to an end with no explanation as to what had occurred downstairs.

The next day dawned clear and bright and brought two new electricians to the Tapestry Room.   The work was completed with no other strange events happening and all was right with the world. The black electrician's tools were collected, as he wouldn't return for them.

Several weeks passed before a representative of the electrical contractor arrived at Pat's door. It took them that long before they found out what happened in

The Tapestry Room Basement, where a ghostly figure was once encountered during a Haunted Lebanon Tour -- and where electricians had weird experiences of their own.

(Left) The original staircase in the Tapestry Room basement where an electrician encountered a mysterious mist that sprouted legs.

(Right) The bricked-over entrance to a tunnel that is located under the staircase.

the basement that fateful night. The room where the electrician had to work on the wiring in was as far back into the basement as you could go. The 12-foot by 12-foot room, which is located under the kitchen, has a small staircase that is original to the building. The staircase was boarded over at some point and is no longer used. Beneath the staircase is something unusual: an entrance to a tunnel. The entrance was bricked up long ago. It has been said that many of Lebanon's downtown business are connected by tunnels. It is also said that there may have been a stop on the Underground Railroad in Lebanon. The Underground Railroad was a series of safe havens for those escaping slavery in the South.

This network seems to be much larger today than it was in the 1800s. Everyone who finds an old barn, a hidden room, or a clearing in the woods that they can't explain thinks that they were part of the Underground Railroad. Not many of the actual sites were well documented, if at all. Earlier, I mentioned the electrician who was working in the basement was black. I only mentioned that because it may have been a trigger for whatever happened when he was down there. If the tunnel was a hiding spot for runaway slaves, having a black man at that location may have started a strange series of events.

Days after the incident, the electrician told his supervisors what happened that night. As he was working in the middle of the small room, the temperature rapidly started to drop. Suddenly, a mist started to form and swirl about three feet from the base of the staircase. As the swirling mist grew larger, it floated a few feet above the stairs. Suddenly, a pair of legs appeared out of the mist and started ascending the staircase. That's when the electrician decided he had seen enough and out he came! Pat told me that he had never seen anyone so scared in all of his life. On hearing this tale, I knew that the game was once again afoot.

It was a Friday night, several years ago that I had picked to investigate the Tapestry Room. Fridays are usually good for assembling the team, but for some reason, almost everyone was busy that night. I did manage to get Luke Naliborski and my old friend and new investigator, Ernie Lingo, to help with the night's events.

We met Pat at the restaurant at 8 p.m. Since it was the middle of January, it was quite dark and unusually quiet in town. I informed Pat about our standard procedures and about how long we would take to complete our tasks. I was to call him when we were done so he could lock up for the night. With the groundwork laid for the evening, Pat left, but not before locking us in the restaurant.

When I assemble the team for an investigation they know the location must be haunted. I don't give them any of the details until their initial walk-through. I want them to get their own impressions of the location and not have any pre-conceived ideas about a place. I walked Luke and Ernie through the restaurant and all around the basement. Then we sat at a table upstairs and I asked for any impressions they might have gathered on their own. We all have the ability to experience paranormal energy if we allow ourselves to open up and let the natural order of things flow. Ernie and Luke both mentioned a feeling of heaviness in the basement. I then filled them in on all I knew about the building that housed the Tapestry Room Restaurant.

It was around 1850 when 123 W. Saint Louis St. was built. With so many styles of architecture to choose from in Lebanon in those days, the Victorian style was chosen for this particular building. The mansard roof, which dominates the structure, wasn't added until 1870.

One of the early owners, Henry Bachmann, operated a hotel here. Henry gave way to his son, Charles, who ran Bachmann's Funeral Parlor and Furniture Store at the site. The funeral parlor was upstairs. A two-story carriage house is located behind the main building. The carriage house is now a garage. The garage's facade gives no indication of its past function.

Christian and Elizabeth Heer bought the building in 1922. The Heers had moved to Lebanon in 1913 and operated a general store at this location until in 1922 they literally swapped sites with Charles Bachmann. The funeral home and furniture store moved into 201-203 W. Saint Louis St. and 123 became the Heer General Store. You could get anything at the general store from a shirt to a live chicken. Antiques and live animals intermingled throughout the store. For 63 years the Heer family operated the store until they retired from business in 1985.

In 1964, the building was given a St. Clair County Historical Landmark Award. In 1978, it was listed on the National Register of Historic Places. The Bachmann family sold the building to Ott Meyer, who ran a funeral home and furniture store there until November of 1940. That is when Meyer, and his wife, Mathilda, moved the funeral parlor to 317 W. St. Louis St., where it is located today. The Cross-Eyed Elephant Antiques can currently be found at 201 W. Saint Louis St. Jenifer Hartman had a consignment shop called Elephant Woods Antiques at 123 for a while before the Tapestry Room was born.

There were plenty of colorful local characters associated with 127 W. St. Louis Street, but nothing traumatic happened there that I could find. Of course, you don't need a tragic event to cause a haunting.

As for the tunnels, I don't believe they have anything to do with the Underground Railroad. Several businesses are supposed to be connected by the tunnels. I can find no one with a definite answer to what function they served, or rock solid proof as to why the tunnels are there. This is a mystery that refuses to be solved.

Now that the team knew all that I did about the location, we decided to try and document some evidence in the basement. Armed with our equipment, we went to the small room in the rear of the basement. The foundation of the building is made up of large blocks of limestone. Now, any of you who have gone on the Alton Hauntings Tours know all about limestone; it has a high quartz content. Breaking everything down to energy, these stones seem to act like a sponge, storing energy like a battery. The stones let go of some of this energy every now and then. Many of the other buildings in Lebanon also have foundations made of limestone.

With the foundation materials were duly noted, the three of us set up our equipment. I aimed my camera at the base of the stairs with the tunnel entrance to the left of the shot. Luke aimed his camera to the right of mine in the doorway of the room. We now had intersecting shots of the same area. Since this was Ernie's first investigation, he nervously stood by and waited until we needed him.

I decided to have Luke stand in the camera shot and ask random questions. I had given Ernie and Luke the general history of the location, but not all the details. This made Luke's questions come from his immediate impressions. Well, Luke wasn't impressing anybody. The three of us were in near- total darkness. We had video cameras with infrared extenders, tape recorders, TriField Meters and thermo - scanners. We had all the equipment, but nothing was happening. It was time to change tactics.

We don't normally ask an entity to move something or manifest itself, as this requires an extreme amount of energy. We may do this after being in a location several times and we believe the entity is benign. Well, we went right for the throat on this one. As Ernie and I stood behind my camera, Luke started the dog and pony show.

Luke: "If anyone is with us now, can you say something?" We were greeted with silence. Our tape recorders, which were voice-activated, did nothing.

Luke: "If there is anyone with us now, could you touch one of us?" We heard the bones in Ernie's back crack as he tightened up upon hearing that request.

Luke: "If there is anyone with us now, can you rap on the wall to let us know you are here?"

Instead of a gentle tap on the wall, it sounded as if the entire upstairs was coming down on our heads. We screamed and scrambled out of the room and into the larger part of the basement. After gathering our composure, I turned on the basement lights and we cautiously re-entered the little room. Not a thing was amiss. The video footage contained nothing, as did the tape recorders. There were only Luke's questions followed by our screams and panicked sounds of a hasty retreat. It seemed like a good time for a break.

Upstairs, in the friendly confines of the well-lit restaurant, we started to relax. It may very well have been the bathroom break that we took that helped us wind down. I was thrilled that I hadn't soiled myself from fright. If the other two had, they were silent on the matter.

As we sat at a table, armed with soft drinks and snacks, I filled the boys in on the rest of the building's history. I knew Luke and Ernie would have been more tentative if they knew it had once been a funeral home. As I talked, I noticed that something seemed to have caught Ernie's attention. Over my shoulder, in the doorway between the restaurant and the gift shop, a wind chime was moving. Not the entire wind chime. As you know, in the middle of the chimes hangs the striker. From that hangs the piece of paper or cloth that is blown by the wind and causes the striker to move. That bottom piece was moving in a slow, clockwise rotation while the rest of the chime was motionless. We circled the wind chime, even putting our hands around it, but could find no reason for the unusual movement. There was no air moving anywhere in the immediate area. As I went to grasp the lower piece of the wind chime, it stopped! I lowered my hand, totally amazed. As I did, the bottom piece started circling again, this time in a counter-clockwise direction.

By this time you would be well within your rights as thinking individuals to ask, "Why didn't you photograph or record this event?" The answer is simple: we had left all our equipment in the basement.

We decided this would be a good time to go back to the basement, if for nothing else than to gather up our toys. It was at this point in our investigation that I noticed that Luke was a bit on edge. Luke is married and all of us married fellows are a bit on edge, but this was different. Luke kept looking behind himself and holding his hand out. It seemed that right after our initial basement encounter, there was a 20-degree cold sport that was following him throughout the building. It was starting to unnerve him. Since nothing was bothering me, I decided to press on.

On re-entering the small basement room, I decided to try one more shot at communication with the unseen force. After all, nothing had happened to me...yet.

We put new film in the cameras and new tapes in the voice recorders. This time, I stood in front of the camera lenses. I should have realized my position. I entered the camera shot with my profile and stayed that way. It looked like the classic opening of "Alfred Hitchcock Presents." But let's forget about my non-chiseled body and keep up with the narrative. I started asking more pointed questions to the unseen force. This time, there were no answers, no touches from unseen hands and no raps on the walls. We decided to call it a night.

I will now repeat myself, as I often do. The most boring part of paranormal investigating is going over the mounds of evidence that is accumulated. I can only do ten minutes at a time or I fall asleep. I was positive that we would have a revelation of some sort, what with the dramatic events of the night. When I got to the part, both on the video and on the tape recording, where Luke asked if whatever was there would rap on the wall not a thing was recorded. That is, not a thing that was paranormal. After Luke's question you could hear the three of us yelling and swearing and running away like scared little schoolgirls. I was devastated by this loss. This was another dramatic event with no evidence.

Kim decided to join me for the rest of the evidence viewing. We were going through the Alfred Hitchcock episode when Kim yelled for me to stop the videotape. I stopped it and then backed it up. Since Kim's hearing is far better than mine, she picked up a voice that I would have missed. When I was in the basement I asked if the entity was connected to the location when it was a funeral home. A distinctive male voice answers, "NO!" The odd part was that the voice was recorded on the videotape, not the tape recorder.

This was my first encounter in the old restaurant, but certainly not my last.

Often, during my forays into Lebanon, I'll pop into a place that I believe is haunted and just tell the proprietor that I'll be in the basement (or whatever location is haunted) for a while. Pat's so used to my impromptu visits to the Tapestry Room that all I have to do is walk in and point to where I'm going. The basement of the building has heaviness to it, a pressure that engulfs you. It doesn't seem to matter whether you are alone or in a group. The deeper you walk into the basement, the eerier it becomes.

Several months after the first investigation, I found myself alone in the basement of the Tapestry Room. It was about 2 p.m. on a Thursday. Outside, the sun was shining and inside the lunch crowd was starting to thin out. I always carry a small flashlight and a disposable camera with me. I never know when I'll need some extra light, thus the flashlight. I prefer a disposable camera for two reasons: the first is that if I do capture something on film, I have a negative to back up the photo. The other reason is that I am extremely clumsy. My clumsiness has been enhanced over the last several years by my worsening physical condition. When I'm not falling over something, I tend to lose my grip on anything in my hands. Thus, many cameras have died in the line of ghostly fire. I can replace disposable cameras at a price I can afford.

As I moved deeper into the basement, the heaviness seemed to envelope me. By the time I made it to the small room in the back of the basement, the pressure in my chest was almost unbearable. Suddenly I was blanketed with total blackness when every light in the basement went out. As this has happened to me in other places, I calmly reached for my flashlight. It wouldn't work! Now I was in a bit of a pickle.

The dining area of the Tapestry Room. Moving furniture, loud crashes and shifting cold spots frequently occur in this area of the building.

I normally like pickles, but this was completely different. Thinking quickly, I realized that I could use my camera as an ally. I've never had a disposable camera fail to flash on command. I pulled the camera out and started taking photos with the flash. Each flash enabled me to get a fix on where I was and I slowly made my way to the staircase that led to the main level. When I got to the top of the stairs, I checked the light switch. It was on, but the lights were off.

I bumped into Pat in the gift shop. He realized right away that something had happened by my expression and pale face. I quickly filled him in as we made our way to the top of the stairs. The light switch was still on, but now all the lights in the basement were functioning. The switch and the lights now appeared to be operating as they should.

I am not the only one who has had other worldly experiences at the Tapestry Room. In the past year there was a problem with the service due to nighttime visitations. A young man who was employed as a cook at the restaurant had an apartment in the rear of the building, behind the kitchen. He was an exceptional employee through his first two weeks on the job. By the third week, however, things started to go awry. At first, small parts of the customers' orders would come out wrong. Then entire orders were screwed up. As the complaints started to mount, Pat asked the cook why he had suddenly lost his touch. The young man explained that he wasn't getting any sleep at night. He said he was bothered by noises from the restaurant. The sounds were quite loud and scary. The cook said it sounded like a barroom brawl, with smashing tables and flying chairs. The dawn always revealed a calm and intact restaurant.

These disturbances have settled down, but little annoyances continue. Moving chairs and the lights going on and off are your basic ghostly fare. One incident that happens every couple of weeks is a bit more disturbing. In the kitchen is a coffee machine with all sorts of bells and whistles. You need a degree from M.I.T. to work this thing. Many a morning, on entering the restaurant, Pat will find the coffee machine doing its thing all over the floor. As always, when checked there is nothing mechanically wrong.

The investigation of the Tapestry Room, like that of many of the locations in Lebanon, is a work in progress. I have documented the hauntings as real but I have been unable to find a historic event to explain what is going on, paranormally. So far, that is!

So, come to the Tapestry Room Restaurant for the wonderful fare. They don't serve alcohol, but be warned; maybe spirits will still be served at your table, cold and free of charge.

TEA FOR TWO?

How many times have you gone into a little cafe with a couple of friends? Another friend is supposed to arrive shortly, so, you get a table with an extra seat. Have you ever had that friend not show, but someone totally unexpected does?

Welcome to The Sweeter House of Coffee, located in the second block of West St. Louis Street. When Pat and Jerry Schwieder opened up a little over a year ago, they had already been warned about my imminent arrival. I had investigated the location several years before when it was The Enchanted Rose tearoom. The teashop opened in 2004. The owners were Scott and Kim Leibovich and Barbara Enders. The shop's intensions, according to the brochure, were to provide a fun and unique atmosphere to celebrate birthdays, births, weddings, anniversaries, or to take a break from the day. Everything from a simple lunch to a Victorian-style tea party could be provided.

Scott Leibovich left his day job as an accountant to become the tearoom's manager. Scott's wife, Kim, and Barb Enders were teachers at La Petite Academy in O'Fallon. Kim left to become a stay-at-home mother. Barb quit teaching to become a truck driver (no really, a truck driver!) After a year had passed, both ladies realized how much they missed all the children. It was decided a tearoom would be a perfect way to create an atmosphere of fun and food for the little ones. Parties could also be arranged for the adults. The parlor was decorated with murals and antiques. Velvet-upholstered furniture filled the room. Dill and cucumber sandwiches and numerous brands of tea were the fare. Hoards of youngsters, dressed in their Victorian finest, partied like it was 1899.

As the owners were new in town, I waited for them to get established before I introduced myself on one of my thrice-weekly walkabouts. Scott informed me that he was told that I was the one to talk to about any strange occurrences in Lebanon. So this top-hatted, frilly-shirted gentleman started to fill me in on the strange happenings at 210 W. St. Louis St.

According to Scott, furniture and small items in the shop would be moved with no explanation. Cold spots were frequently encountered. In the kitchen, tea packets would fly off the shelves. All this was standard ghostly hijinks but a stranger tale was the story of the phantom tea party. All the tea sold at the shop was of the best quality. This was not the cheap stuff sold in grocery stores. Each cup was individually brewed and served up piping hot. Nothing was pre-made. One bright and sunny Sunday morning, on

The Sweeter House of Coffee

entering the store, Kim and Scott's happy mood turned suddenly sour. In the front section of the parlor, where the love seat and coffee table were located, someone had had a nocturnal tea party! The silver tray on the table contained some brewed tea, which had been poured into four small cups. Linen napkins and spoons were also on the table and appeared to have been used. Kim and Scott's anger at first was strictly monetary. You just don't brew and then waste an expensive product! Their anger soon turned to puzzlement when they realized that they and Barb were the only ones with keys to the place, and they knew Barb wouldn't waste precious tea leaves. Who had thrown themselves a tea party and how did they get in?

Barb was out of town. Scott and Kim could account for each other's whereabouts. The three owners were naturally upset about the happenings in their tea parlor. I, on the other hand, went into Scooby Doo mode. That's right, I said

Scooby Doo! Come on, you remember how, every episode, Fred would say, "Well gang, it looks like we have a mystery on our hands." I just had to call my gang to inform them of our mystery.

I had already done my initial investigation and could find no reason for the strange occurrences. Because Lebanon is a college town, the weekends can be a bit noisy. With this in mind, I chose a weeknight for the investigation. Also, with it being in the middle of the week, and with team members having jobs, I could only convince Julie Warren and Bill Alsing to help me. Julie has an extended family that keeps her plate quite full. She also lives about an hour north of Lebanon, so her coming to help me was greatly appreciated. Julie is the voice of reason during an investigation when my wife, Kim, isn't around. She makes sure I follow procedure and that I don't go off on a tangent.

Bill Alsing, as you know, owns the History and Hauntings Bookstore in Alton. Bill's help is always invaluable, even though he has a serious problem. Bill is as quiet as a church mouse! You don't realize that he has wandered off to do video or take photos. Then, when you least expect it, Bill emerges out of the shadows, almost giving you heart failure. I swear I'm going to put a cowbell around his neck.

Getting back to the story, Julie, Bill and I met Scott and Kim Leibovich on the Wednesday night in question. It was a crisp winter evening. There was hardly any traffic, or other street noise for that matter. Scott and Kim locked the three of us in and promised to come back in a couple of hours. I like to let my team members wander around the premises and see if they can pick up any vibes. Julie remarked how the front parlor area seemed chilly, and for lack of a better word, occupied. Bill, like me, noticed nothing unusual. I filled them in on the occurrences that Scott had told me about and we planned our attack. Julie would sit in the front area with camera in hand and try and see if she could make any contact. I wanted Bill to wander through the rest of the upstairs to see if he could scare anything up. I would go into the basement. Kim and Barb had told me that the area at the top of the basement stairs actually frightened them. They always had the feeling of someone standing there. It got so bad that they installed an interior door to block that space from the kitchen. Unfortunately, they would still have to pass the stairs to get to the bathroom. I guess if you're going to get the crap scared out of you, what better place than a bathroom?

With walkie-talkie in hand I descended the stairs, after using the bathroom of course! The basement was a dungeon of dampness, ductwork and dirt. All the electrical wiring around me made my TriField Meter a liability. I set up my video camera and tape recorder. Now it was time to check out the entire basement. The thermo-scanner readings were constant and normal. While scanning the area nothing seemed out of place or felt unusual from my vantage point. As I glanced into the far, rear corner of the basement, my spider-sense started to tingle. A small concrete ramp led to a pile of lumber stacked against one wall. I felt like there was something I needed to see behind that lumber. I moved the lumber I discovered its secret: a large freight elevator was behind the lumber pile. The elevator had no door, but being in the cellar there really was no need of one. You didn't have to be a rocket scientist to see that this elevator hadn't worked in many a year. Broken and rusted gears attested to its long inactivity. I felt a tingly sensation run through me as I stepped into and then and out of the elevator. Still, nothing appeared out to be wrong.

Returning upstairs, I found the gang's results were no better than mine. As we sat wondering what to do next, I noticed a doll dressed in Victorian clothing sitting in a flower-decked swing   suspended from the ceiling. What drew my attention was that it was rotating in a clockwise direction. The rest of the dolls excluding this one were dead still. On further examination we could find no reason for this doll to be spinning. There were no fans operating and the furnace ducts were too far away. As I moved my hands towards the doll to check for moving air, it stopped dead! This happened one other time that night and we cannot explain why.

When it was about time for Scott to return and let us out, I decided to collect my gear from the basement. Halfway down the stairs, I swear that I could hear the elevator running! Well, running is what I did, straight down to the elevator. Northing moved as far as I could see. I replayed my tape and got nothing. On reviewing the video I did get what appeared to be moving lights in the general area of the elevator, but nothing concrete.

I informed Scott that we would review our findings and get back to him as soon as we could. When Julie and Bill and I went over our video and still photos we were astonished to realize that nothing unusual came out on our film. Even the photos of the moving doll appeared still and perfectly normal.

Now, as all legitimate paranormal investigators know, once we established the presence of strange activity, we research the history of the location. I like to focus on not only what business operated there or family resided there; I try to look for personalities that stood out in a historical context.

One of the most memorable eras for 210 W. Saint Louis St. was when Smitty's Market was in business there from 1938 into the 1960s. Fordyce "Smitty" Smith arrived in Lebanon in the late 1930s to manage the old Kroger Store, which was located where the St. Louis Street Café is today. In 1938, Smith opened his own store at 210 W. Saint Louis St. I am drawn to "Smitty" Smith for several reasons. First of all, he was known as good storyteller. When you entered his market you were there for the social interaction as well as the merchandise. Secondly, he was very active in community affairs. Smitty served on the city's zoning board, the school board and he was a member of the volunteer fire department. Thirdly, (and this is my favorite), he was one of the founding members of the Looking Glass Playhouse Community Theater. Smitty came up with the theater's name and served as its first president.

Smitty was a charitable man. Longtime residents remember his yellow station wagon making the rounds during Christmas when he would donate food to the less fortunate. Now, I am not saying that Smitty haunts his old store. I just wanted to share some information I uncovered on a truly beloved Lebanon personality.

Another shop that was located at 210 W. Saint Louis St. was the Robin's Nest. The Robin's Nest was a floral shop that operated about 25 years ago. I have not been able to contact the owners. I did come up with a story from that time from a mutual friend that will be featured prominently later on.

Our mutual friend is Janet Schmitt. She is the owner of the Legendary Creations gift shop in Lebanon. One day, as I was chatting with Janet, I mentioned some of the ghostly occurrences at The Enchanted Rose. When I got to the part about the elevator she stopped me cold. Janet told me that when it was a florist shop, the owner said that on an average of once a week she would hear the elevator running as though it was moving from the basement up to the first floor. Always, on inspection, the rusted, broken, hulk of the elevator had never moved. I now knew that some of the ghostly happenings had been going on for years.

As I continued to make my tri-weekly rounds through Lebanon, Scott or Kim never failed to fill me in on the strange goings-on that just wouldn't stop in the tearoom. A young waitress who was hired to help with the parties seemed to become a target. The beleaguered waitress told me of a time that she ran screaming out of the kitchen as packets of tea flew off the shelf over her head. Taps on the shoulder or fingers running through the hair on the back of her head often announced the ghostly presence.

Alas, in these most difficult of times, The Enchanted Rose Tearoom closed its doors. As with so many small businesses, there just weren't enough customers to serve. I still run into Scott every now and then. He and Kim have opened a shop in another town and things seem to be going well for them. I wish them both nothing but the best of luck.

Now, back to the beginning of our story. I had mentioned that when The Sweeter House of Coffee opened for business, the owners, Pat and Jerry, had been warned about me. As they were preparing for opening day, I arrived and introduced myself. I only mentioned my connection with the community theater but both immediately smiled. They knew I was the ghost guy. I gave them a little history of the building, leaving out the ghost stories. Laughing, they told me that if anything weird happened, they'd let me know. Just for the record, The Sweeter House of Coffee makes the best hot chocolate in the world! Now, where was I? Oh, yes. One day I popped in to visit with Pat during the lull between breakfast and lunch. At that time, the coffeehouse had been open about six months. Pat informed me that she couldn't take it any longer and had to tell me what happened.

She asked me if I remembered the mural on the back wall of the tearoom. I said I did, because I thought it was kind of weird. The mural consisted of two figures facing each other as if in conversation. One morning Pat and a friend arrived early to paint the interior of the shop. As they set their paint cans down in the front of the mural, they laughed about covering up the garden scene, as they didn't care for it at all. When they straightened up after setting down the cans, they screamed in union as the seated figures in the mural were now seated sideways and staring at them! They both did what any normal people would and ran from the room. Summoning their courage they reentered. The mural was now back to its original form. Pat shot a picture of the mural with her camera phone. Both she and her friend then slopped several coats of paint over the offenders. Nothing unusual appeared in the cell phone photo and nothing has bled through the wall since the mural was covered.

I believed the coffeehouse would stay active because it caters to a younger crowd. The local college provides a ready source of clientele and staff.

As some of the young folks have gotten to know me, they are relating tales of their own. Invisible fingers stroking their hair, whispers and taps on the shoulders are a common occurrence. I believe that the energy given off by the younger set is helping to keep the old place alive. Alive with the dead, that is!

Just recently a staff member told me of a frightening experience in the kitchen. As she and a co-worker were preparing a meal, a can of Pam cooking spray flew across the kitchen. It flew, and then so did they: right out of there.

As I was gathering the new information from the workers, Pat came in the room with a puzzled look. For weeks she has been trying to track down a strange noise that seems to come from the basement. It only happens every now and then. She told me it sounded like an elevator, but then, what would an elevator be doing in the building? I then informed her that there most certainly was an elevator in the place. Of course it hasn't run in many years and will never move again. Once Pat regained her composure, she told me that I was now going to be on her speed dial. You know, "WHO YOU GONNA CALL?"

The Sweeter House of Coffee, like many other sites in Lebanon, seems to have an otherworldly life. I have investigated many of the locations in Lebanon and believe them to be genuinely haunted. My only problem is I don't know by whom or what. A great deal of the energy seems to be residual. If there is an intelligence there, I believe it holds no ill feelings towards anyone...at least for now.

ALL THE ETHEREAL WORLD'S A STAGE

To take a leisurely stroll down the main street of Lebanon is to step back into another time, another place. While gazing at the old storefronts, it isn't hard to travel back to a simpler time of clean air, friendly neighbors and no cell phones.

Scientists have found that suspension of the present, or daydreaming, is quite healthy for the mind. Nowhere else in Lebanon can the present take a vacation, and your senses soar through the world of make-believe, than at the Looking Glass Playhouse Community Theater. This grand old theater has been a venue for everything from silent movies to a stage production of "Titanic."

The Looking Glass Playhouse Community Theater originated at McKendree College. In March of 1972, a graduate of the college, Shirley Schaefer, volunteered to help the school raise much-needed capital by directing and producing a musical. Local newspapers put out the casting call and the flood of actors, musicians, scene-builders, painters and gophers (I actually mean Go-fors, as in, go for coffee) came pouring in. The Rodgers and Hammerstein musical, "Carousel," was on its way. The show was so successful that a second musical, "Fiddler on the Roof," soon followed.

The two productions made a tidy profit of $6,000 for the college. This was quite a sum of money at the time. Shirley and her intrepid band of followers wondered why they couldn't make this a reality on a consistent basis. The seeds of the theater had been sown!

On August 20, 1973, at the Schaefer home on Mary Jane Street, Shirley, Smitty Smith, Mary Pennington, Raymond Devey, Betty Kaufman, Ruth Schaefer, Dick Boyd, Dona Monroe, Beth Larson, Joan Pocereva, Marianna Davis, Judy Baehr, Jo Giger, Carson Hemper, and Norbert Krausz gathered to create the Looking Glass Theater. The name was taken from that of the prairie, which is located east of

The Looking Glass Playhouse

Lebanon and is mentioned in Charles Dickens book, "American Notes."

The organization's vision was to turn the playhouse into the cultural mecca of the Metro-East area. Another objective was to make live theater available to children. As the saying goes, "The children are our future," and it was felt that they needed to have the opportunity to experience live theater, both on and off the stage.

The first order of business for the leadership of the Looking Glass Playhouse was to file for incorporation with the state of Illinois. Because the group was brand new, this caused a bit of a problem.

The board of directors had a treasurer, but no money. Secretary Ruth Schaefer stepped up to the plate and lent the other founders $25.00 to get the ball rolling. Membership cards were drawn up and the train was roaring down the track. The problem was, the train didn't have a station.

The Alamo theater in downtown Lebanon had been sitting empty for several years. Now, this is where a hint of controversy comes up. There were actually two theaters in town. One was called the Arcade and the other was the Alamo. The names have been batted back and forth by the locals as to which one was the town's original theater. I've mentioned on numerous occasions that researching the history of Lebanon is like investigating a car accident. If 10 folks see the same accident, they will have 10 different versions of what happened. As so much of Lebanon's history is oral, I've gotten a world of different versions of the town's rich history.

I believe that Lebanon's original theater was the Arcade, located on West St. Louis Street where Pearson's Print Shop is today. Pearson's is a brand new building as the theater burnt down years ago. There may have been an arcade on site as well, thus the name. I came across an advertisement for the theater in a copy of The Lebanon *Advertiser* from 1918. During further research I came across an article about a place called The Sun theater. It seems to have been in the same location as the Arcade. Silent movies were listed as the fare for the day. Both names could belong to the same place. Again, different people I've interviewed have had different recollections of the same location and events.

I have a photo of the front of the current Looking Glass Playhouse from the late 1920s. The local electrical utility had an office in the building and the employees posed out front for a picture. Across the top of the open entrance, etched into the building, is the word "Alamo." As far as I know, the Looking Glass Playhouse site has

The front of the Alamo Theater in the early 1920s. Local utility workers, who had an office in the back of the building, pose in front of the theater.

always been called the Alamo. Land plats that I have obtained from The University of Illinois don't show a theater at the corner of West St. Louis Street and St. Clair until the late 1920s. Before that, and my paperwork goes back to 1894, there was a single family residence on that spot. Eventually, the family moved from the house on the corner and it became the offices for The Lebanon Journal newspaper. Whether the newspaper was profitable or not is a moot point. Its greatest claim to fame came in 1919 when the building burned down in a spectacular blaze. Onlookers' final impression of the inferno was seeing the printing press falling from the upper level into the basement as the flooring turned to ash.

By the late 1920s, the Alamo theater rose phoenix-like from the ashes. The theater was a mainstay of the city for years as silent movies gave way to the talkies. But alas, the days of the small local movie houses were numbered. As subdivisions spawned malls and shopping plazas, cineplexes came to life. These leviathans crushed the life out of the small local theaters. Soon these little oases of local culture fell silent. This explains why in 1973 the Alamo was sitting vacant, covered in dust, and waiting for someone to show it a little love and respect. In came the newly formed Looking Glass Playhouse or LGP. The vacant building would be a perfect venue for live theater, with a little love and a lot of elbow grease.

The group convinced the building's owner, Cleve C. Weyenberg, to lease the theater for $50 a month. Of course, this would start after the first play's receipts came in. On Labor Day of 1973, the "Great Labor Day Cleanup" began. The building, which had been empty for years, was getting a cleaning on a massive scale. Years of dust were removed. The original bathrooms in the basement were cleaned and sanitized. Anything that could be salvaged became a theater prop. The dream was becoming a reality.

On November 2, 1973, the Looking Glass Playhouse opened with the production of "Babes in Toyland." It would have been a packed house even without anyone showing up to watch the performance, as there were 125 people in the cast. The actors ranged in age from 5 to 60. The production was almost like a 3-D show as the small stage caused the performers to be literally in the audience members' laps. All else aside, the three performances of "Babes" managed to turn a small profit. The theater was on its' way! To help supplement the plays, concerts were held between performances. With no lobby, popcorn was popped and bagged down the street at "Moonie" Monroe's house. Teenagers would then run the bags of popcorn to the theater and sell them, along with candy, seat by seat.

In March of 1974, the stage was enlarged and wings were added that allowed the stagehands to move props into position during the show. Before this, the show had to be literally stopped to reset for each scene. The auditorium floor sloped down to the stage, as all movie theaters do. This caused a small problem for Marilyn Boyd, who was the accompanist for the production. The floor, being tilted, caused the piano and its bench to be tilted, also. During some of the shows' big musical numbers, it was a chore for Marilyn to keep from sliding off the bench and ending up on the floor. A riser was later added to prevent such an occurrence.

Other problems arose during the productions. The patrons seemed to enjoy musicals more the straight shows. When the LGP Players moved into the theater many of the seats were missing. Chairs had to be donated and seats were hauled up from the basement but there never seemed to be enough. As crowds flocked the theater for "South Pacific," chairs had to be borrowed from McKendree College. The crowds, though welcome, caused more problems for the aging building. The original restrooms were downstairs with access from a narrow staircase. The old plumbing couldn't handle the numerous requests and one restroom shut down completely. The remaining facility now became a common room for all. Broken pipes caused costumed performers to take turns mopping the floors when not on stage.

I've always said that the best parts of every show are the things that the audience never sees. The long rehearsals and the backstage tragedies reveal those who truly love the theater. My good friend, Gigi Dowling Urban, told me during my first show at The LGP in 1997 that the easiest part of the theater was being on stage. Truer words were never spoken!

In August of 1974, the front east apartment was converted into a concession area. A canopy was also added to the front entrance.

October of 1974 saw the playhouse come alive with the living dead. The Halloween exhibit was called "A Visit to Transylvania." It was the first spook house of its kind in the area. It cost 50 cents to see Dracula rise from his coffin and run amok in the theater. While entertaining for the masses, it took quite a bit of work to put everything back together for the second night. During the second night, a basement wall collapsed and the show was shut down. Talk about bringing down the house!

In March of 1975, the Looking Glass Players brought "Mame" to the stage. By then, new restrooms had been installed upstairs in the concession area. One bathroom was a converted closet and the other had been there from when the area was an apartment. "Mame" was such a success that the large crowds strained the plumbing and the sewers overflowed all over the basement. Costumed performers became plumbers and custodians when not on stage. Due to the flooding, performers had to change clothes outside the stage doors, hanging costumes on tree limbs. The night performances weren't a problem; the matinees caused more than one motorist to almost have an accident.

The first attempts at buying the building from Cleve Weyenberg came in 1975. Weyenberg wanted $40,500. The building was appraised at $30,000.

By late 1977, the Looking Glass Playhouse was being dealt a double blow. The rent kept increasing, and with rising utility costs, it now cost approximately $500 a month to keep operations running smoothly. Also, the founding members had been sacrificing time and energy for four years. It was now time for others to step up to the plate.

In 1978, the LGP's fifth anniversary, Dona Monroe was elected as the first woman president of the board of directors. Dona's first order of business was to appoint a building committee to search out ways to either buy the theater or find another venue that would suit their needs. Mimi Kuhn was the head of the committee and an escrow account was set up to get the ball rolling.

The aged theater seemed to be falling down all around them. The leaky roof caused buckets to be placed on stage, even during performances. A combination of large crowds and heavy rains caused flooded sewers in the basement. Winter performances saw actors and patrons alike bundled up against the cold as smoke and mirrors held an ancient furnace together. The air conditioning unit died and made the summer productions almost unbearable from the heat. At this time, if the audience became bored with the production, they could watch what was going on in the basement through gaping holes in the floor. The theater was a jumble of wiring. Some of the wiring was traceable, some of it wasn't. When microphones were used, police calls would come over the loud speakers. Theater seats, already a problem, were dismantled in the front rows in order to scavenge parts for the rest of the chairs. On several occasions, ticket sellers sold seats that weren't even there! Because the stage was so small, performers had to exit the theater to go to the dressing rooms in the basement. The "dressing rooms" consisted of nails in the wall on which to hang costumes.

In November of 1978, Sandi O'Neal, wife of the then-lieutenant governor of Illinois, took a bit part in "Man of La Mancha." Her political status brought much-needed publicity to the playhouse.

On June 5, 1979, the Looking Glass Playhouse received a non-profit tax number, largely due to the efforts of Tony Ptacek.

By 1980, the building fund had reached $5,000. A special meeting was held on March 12 to discuss buying the playhouse building. By then, the asking price had risen to $55,500. Twenty-five percent, or $11,500, would be required for a bank loan. The theater's total assets were only $12,800. Renovations would cost another $5,000. On July 21, 1980, the board agreed to purchase the theater building for $44,000. Negotiations continued. On November 22, 1980, ownership of the theater became a reality. A bottle of champagne was broken over the corner of the building by former president Dona Monroe. Now that ownership of the theater was no longer just a dream, and money had been borrowed for improvements, a time frame for construction needed to be set. The theater would be dark (no shows running) from late May through early October 1981. This was to become volunteer labor at its finest. Everything that was to be saved was stored in barns. The back wall of the building was torn down and a 40-foot addition was added which went all the way to the back alley. The basement was extended the length of the building. The roof was replaced, as was the damaged ceiling. The old light booth was torn down and replaced. A catwalk was installed in the rafters to set lights and improve the electrical quality of the building. The furnace and air conditioner were moved downstairs, which cut the noise dramatically. The J. R. Mueller Construction Company did the rebuilding, with many of the men donating their time on nights and weekends. Volunteers came from far and wide to clean and paint.

Under the guidance of Gigi Dowling and the Fundraising Committee, funds were raised for the building additions, outside normal theater income.

By August, performers were able to access the stage for the first time without having to go outside first. Some members of the local Rotary Club took it upon themselves to decorate the front of the building while others toiled inside. The Rotarians then moved inside to paint the lobby and concession areas.

Fundraisers -- a theater staple -- abounded, and by 1983, the Looking Glass Playhouse celebrated its tenth anniversary in style.

In February of 1984, a longstanding problem was finally remedied. The Ritz Theater, an old movie house in Greenville, Ill., donated 400 seats to the playhouse. Volunteers from Lebanon piled into trucks of all shapes and sizes and grabbed every available chair from the Ritz. It was very fortunate that the new seats were donated, as heating and cooling costs for the now-larger structure were rising at an alarming rate.

In July, volunteers from the Freeburg Carpenters' Union, Local #480, laid new flooring in the theater. The new seats were then installed.

I'll assume that many of you are like me when it comes to the theater. I love the danger of live theater, whether on stage or watching from the auditorium. If there is a screw-up, you had better be prepared to cover and go with the flow. This being understood, a performance of a show cannot be 100 percent under your control. A good case in point occurred in October of 1984. The Friday night audience of "The Music Man" got more than they bargained for when they bought their tickets. Right before the performance started, firemen rushed in and ushered everyone into the basement. Apparently, a tornado was on the way! Thirty tense minutes went by before the all clear was sounded. You know what they say: "THE SHOW MUST GO ON!" and it did, without a hitch.

In September of 1985, The Illinois Arts Council made its first grant to the Looking Glass Playhouse for $4,105. September also brought about the costume room being moved to the former second floor east apartment. The constant flooding downstairs was ruining the costumes.

November of 1985 saw President Tony Ptacek push for a new light board for the theater. It seemed that "ghost" lights were now becoming a problem. Julie Kuhn, chairwoman of the light committee, reported that the lights had a life of their own. Lights would stay on when switched off and fadeouts were impossible. As much as I would love to blame something paranormal, the theater's maze of untraceable wires may have had something to do with the electrical nightmare. A new light board was installed in February 1986. That year also brought secure fire doors and new carpeting.

The beginning of 1988 saw bleak times for the theater's pocketbook. A decline in fundraising and grants almost exhausted the bank account. By the end of 1988, with a new grant from the Illinois Arts Council, and a season of can't miss shows, the Playhouse returned to being financially stable.

One of the Looking Glass Playhouse's most beloved fundraisers was initiated in 1989. Director Don Urban brought Charles Dickens' "A Christmas Carol" to life. This heart-warming tale brings joy to countless patrons every holiday season.

To this day, hundreds of talented folks have graced the stage of the Looking Glass Playhouse. Not everyone has been employed on stage. Many have pumped life back into the old place with the use of other talents, such as, painting, sawing, carpentry, financial wizardry, and good, hard volunteer labor. The best way I can think of to sum up the historical section of our tale is to quote the Looking Glass Playhouse's historian, Dona Monroe. In February, 1990, she wrote: "The Looking Glass Playhouse continues to be a viable part of the community and is growing as an established and important community theater in the Metro-east and indeed in the southwestern Illinois area. Generally members of the audience come to the Playhouse from a 50- to 75-mile radius surrounding Lebanon, and word of mouth is still the LGP's best source of advertising. The lifeblood of the Looking Glass Playhouse is its members, whose creativity on and off the stage provide cultural experiences for audience and participants alike. Hundreds of these people have worked in and for the Looking Glass Playhouse during its formation and growth, and the historian apologizes for not being able to mention each and every one of them."

Now in 2008, the Looking Glass Playhouse still isn't resting on its laurels. Major renovations have taken place over the last several years that have added to the comfort and security of its patrons and performers. New concession and ticket areas have been installed. New modern bathrooms have made intermissions less exciting. A new dressing room and workshop are being installed as I write. The Looking Glass Playhouse has been the guiding light of Community Theater in southern Illinois for 35 years. Its mission from the beginning was to be a leader, and it still is to this day."

In the introduction to this book, I described my coming to Lebanon and my baptism in the local theater. Even though my physical capabilities are deteriorating, I have been able to stay quite active at the old LGP. While my onstage appearances and my custodial duties are ebbing, my involvement in other areas, such as the board of directors, theater historical research, and ambassador at large, keep me very busy. I am the current board vice-president, but before being a board member at all, I was one of the maintenance crew along with my good buddy, Ernie Lingo. So that no one gets offended I just want to state that Ernie and I are in charge of maintenance in title only. To be a member of the Playhouse involves far more than being on stage. During my first show in 1998, assistant director Gigi Dowling Urban told me that acting on stage was the easiest part of community theater. Boy, was she right! So much more is involved with running a show and more importantly, running the day-to-day functions of the theater. Many dedicated people have shaped, promoted, constructed and cleaned the old LGP before Ernie and I, and hopefully many will long after we're gone.

Having the maintenance titles allows Ernie and I to have keys to the entire building. All board members have keys, but only to their respective areas of concern. Ernie and I can roam at will! I have spent many hours, often long into the night as a board member, but more often in a custodial capacity. These projects have left me alone in the massive structure on more than one occasion. I should say that in body I was alone, in spirit I was one of a very large cast.

One of the oldest adages in the world of entertainment is that any theater worth its salt has a ghost. I believe the Looking Glass Playhouse has a full saltshaker. I have had numerous encounters of the paranormal variety at the theater. Being a paranormal investigator, I've tried to find a logical explanation for each and every occurrence. I've only been able to explain half of them. As I stated earlier, my many maintenance projects have gone late into the evenings when rehearsals are over and I am alone in the theater. Some simple projects quickly changed and took on a life of their own. Ernie and I keep a clipboard in the front of the theater that allows members to jot down anything that needs our attention. When each project is completed it is checked off the list. Several years ago, the list informed me that the florescent bulbs in the downstairs ladies dressing room needed to be replaced. Ernie and I fought viciously over who got that one! Not really, but it makes a better story. Actually, I was the first one to see it on the list, and because it was a simple project, I decided to give the girls the light they so richly deserved. I was still working at the time. For those of you who don't know my story, I'm permanently disabled from a severe back injury and a resulting condition that keeps me in constant pain and has complicated every function of my body. I've accepted the cards that have been dealt me. Nobody ever said that life was fair. I believe that life is what you make it, be that good or bad. But I digress. I used to get off from work in the middle of the afternoon. My wife, Kim, wouldn't be home for hours from her job in the wonderful world of retail, so I decided to swing by the old theater and see what projects I could tackle. Most of the jobs on the list were going to involve a small army, but thankfully, I could handle changing some light bulbs. Oh, was I wrong!

The main lights in the ladies' dressing room are suspended from the ceiling in the middle of the room. It's one large 14-foot by 14-foot room with multiple sinks and two small enclosed toilet areas. The ceiling was low enough for me to use a metal folding chair and not have to track down a ladder. While standing on the chair, I noticed that the two long bulbs of the light fixture were protected on the outside by a thin, transparent sheet of plastic. Each end of the plastic sheet had a decorative screw that held the plastic in place. The screws could be removed by hand. I had not yet had my carpal tunnel surgery (I was actually two years from that) but I was starting to have trouble in certain capacities with my hands.

While I was taking out the second screw, it flipped out of my hand and hit the metal chair I was standing on before making its way to the floor. I heard it land, but I didn't see the screw. I figured it couldn't have gone far. I picked the chair up and tilted it to make sure the screw wasn't there. After placing the chair next to the door,

I got on my hands and knees and scoured the area. I was not happy to find that the screw had vanished. This was a specialty screw and I hate to rig things up with improper hardware. I replaced the bulbs and checked the area one more time for the missing hardware. Having no luck, I decided to look for a replacement part. I spent about 15 minutes down the hallway where our shelves of nails, screws, and assorted treasures are kept. I found a screw I thought might work and returned to the dressing room. In the fifteen minutes I was gone, the room had changed. The metal folding chair that I had used for a ladder had moved from the dressing room doorway to the center of the room. On approaching the chair I noticed something shiny in the middle of the seat. It was th screw that I had been searching for! Being the legendary paranormal investigator that my ego and the voices in my head, tell me I am, I backtracked. Going down the list I knew I had checked my clothing, the chair and the floor for the screw. I had left the chair by the doorway after replacing the bulbs. Something odd was going on here. I searched the downstairs area and called out to anyone who may have come into the building without my knowledge. I was alone. On my return to the dressing room, while I was standing on the chair, replacing the light cover, it suddenly got very cold in the room. My first reaction was to exclaim something unprintable but being the trouper I am, or being too scared to run, I simply thanked whoever was there for the assistance and then I finished putting the light together.

My work was through, but my curious nature was stirred, not shaken. Not being able to resist, I asked whatever entity was there to move the chair. I know it's first grade, but I couldn't resist. Of course nothing happened. It was time to go home. On my way out the door I thanked whoever had assisted me. This was not my first encounter, nor would it be my last.

I have had more experiences in the theater than I can count using both hands, both feet, and my, well, a lot! Although the hauntings range throughout the entire theater my favorite happening occurred, again, in the dressing room area.

We all know that October is Fire Safety Month throughout the United States. This past October I was sitting at one of the makeup tables in the basement. Spread out before me was every smoke detector the theater owned. It was time to change the batteries and be up to code until spring arrived. It was early on a Saturday morning and I was the only one in the theater. I was listening to the Beatles on my iPod, in other words, I was lost in my own little world. Suddenly the air around me became freezing cold and a young girl's voice came through the iPod's earphones. The song stopped and I heard the voice ask, "What are you doing?" Still not putting two and two together (math never was my strong suit), I turned to see who had come into the dressing room. It was then that I realized I was still alone, that is, I was the only one visible. I took off the earphones and calmly explained what I was doing. The frigid air warmed after about thirty seconds. Because I believe the theater's entities to be friendly, I just went back to what I was doing. I've tested the iPod on numerous occasions and the song that was playing during the episode plays right through without a hitch.

I am happy to say that I've made many good friends over the years that are well respected in the field of the paranormal. Not one of them has had, or has heard of, an episode with an iPod. Finally, I am first at something!

With a theater of this size and so many stories to tell, I feel that it would be easier to go through it all by location, rather than worry about timelines. Keeping that in mind, we'll stick with the downstairs dressing room area. During the run of a show this place is alive with activity. Performers sit at two long multi-lighted tables, applying makeup and running over lines in their minds. The dressing rooms are a tornado of flying costumes and local show gossip. The downstairs hallway, aka "the tunnel," is a stream of technicians and actors making their way to designated points. Stored off the sides of the tunnel are building supplies, old flats, portable fireplaces, antique refrigerators, and assorted large props. The end of the hallway contains the small prop area and the original bathrooms from the theater's movie era. The current workstation is located in the corner of the makeup/sitting area. This is a beehive of activity during a show's production and quite a lonely area during the few respites of the year. The St. Clair Street dressing room doors are used mainly by theater personnel because the theater patrons use the front doors. This seems to be my main entrance.

It often happens that even though paranormal investigators are constantly searching for signs of the beyond, we are rarely prepared when something really good happens. A couple of months before my encounter in the ladies' dressing room (Wow, that sounds bad!), I was driving by the theater on a bright, clean, holiday morning. I'm usually up hours before Kim, so I go to the theater to check on things. This particular morning, I noticed the side dressing room entrance door standing open about a foot or so. My first reaction was that someone had broken into the theater. Being the brave soul that I am, or idiot, whichever you prefer, I entered the theater through the open door. First, I checked the door for damage. Nothing was wrong and the door mechanism was actually locked. I assumed the door just wasn't closed properly the night before, but I wanted to be sure. I needed to check out the interior of the theater to make sure no one was there.

My only problem was that the theater was completely dark and I had no flashlight with me. I am more familiar now with the location of all the light switches than I was then. Anyone who knows me knows that I possess the poorest night vision ever. My often-bloodied and battered shins are a testament to this sad fact. I found the light switch next to the side door then closed the door so no one could enter the premises. I then proceeded to stumble and trip my way through the dressing rooms, the tunnel, and the small prop area. Then I took the stairs from the old bathroom location to the main floor. Performers who have to make entrances from the back of the theater use these stairs. They were also, obviously, used by the former moviegoers and early LGP patrons to reach the old bathrooms. After searching the first floor foyer, I made my way to the second floor, which contains the costume rooms (formerly small apartments) and the sound booth. The costume rooms, before they were totally rebuilt, were eerie storage places of vintage clothing and costumes. What was eerie about the clothing is that theater patrons donated most of the items after a loved one had passed away. I've come across items with spirits attached and it often made me wonder about some of the things in the theater. The costume area was thankfully void of human activity. I then made my way to the sound booth. This was the old projection booth when the LGP was a movie house. It is also our access to the attic and catwalks. The catwalks have always been scary for me because of the height, nothing paranormal.

I flicked on the lights and made my search from the doorway. When no one responded to my calls, I turned off the attic lights and latched the door. I then proceeded down the steps and into the light booth. The light booth is like the bridge of a ship. All commands come from there. I glanced over the railing and called out into the darkened theater below. My answer was silence. I then went to the far end of the light booth and peered into the electrical closet. There was nothing but panel boxes and wires in there. I was almost done with my search. As I was leaving the sound booth I couldn't remember if I had shut the door to the electrical closet. Turning at the bottom of the staircase towards the electrical closet I let out a scream and jumped back! The area that I had just searched now contained the large figure of a man standing at the door and facing directly towards me. I was now trembling and huddled against the wall at the base of the stairs. Most people would run in this situation. I was getting mad! This was my theater and no one was going to be there unlawfully. Gathering my courage, and making sure I hadn't soiled myself, I lunged past the stairs and towards the panel room. After bumping into the door, it soon became apparent that I was alone. It didn't take a rocket scientist to realize that now would be a good time to leave. The hardest part was turning the lights out behind me. With trembling hands I accomplished that feat of courage and hurriedly made my way downstairs to the foyer.

The only spots in the theater left to inspect were the auditorium and stage. These just happen to be the largest areas in the theater. At least I knew where the lights were and believe me, they all came on. Up and down the rows of seats I went searching for intruders. By this time a human body of any kind would have been welcome. Finding not a soul, I searched the stage area. Many other theater groups envy the Looking Glass Playhouse because of the massive back stage area. This forest of flats has housed large orchestras and huge casts during major musicals. Thankfully, it's also an open space. This part of the search took only a minute or two.

Although somewhat shaken by my earlier encounter, I was satisfied that no living being had trespassed upon our hallowed ground. I then started to backtrack, turning lights out along the way. The upstairs was already done so I didn't have to worry about those. From the stage, through the theater, then down the back staircase I went, darkening the theater room by room. The last light switch was next to the side entrance door. As I reached for it something new grabbed hold of my senses. The sound of four or five people walking around in hard-soled shoes echoed from the stage floor above. How could this be? I was just there! I walked through the darkened makeup area to the staircase that leads up to the back of the stage. The footsteps were loud and imposing. My need to know overwhelmed me. As I took my first step upwards, the footsteps stopped. Should I go farther? Should I turn around and run? What should I do? I decided to yell up the stairs. On receiving no reply I decided that no reply was a good reply. I hurried to the back door, made sure it was locked, and slammed it behind me. With my heart racing I drove home. Thankfully I was back in the sunlight, in the warm world of the living.

During the late 1990s, when I was just starting out at the LGP, my main focus was on stage. One of the many wonderful productions that I've had the great fortune to be a part of was "To Kill a Mockingbird." My role was that of Heck Tate, the town sheriff. Every production goes through four or five weeks of rehearsals, followed by two long weekends (Thursday to Sunday) of shows. This was a fairly large cast and all was calm and serene, that is, paranormal-wise, until the second weekend. During the second act of the show my character was the first person on the witness stand. After that, I could pretty much daydream, while throwing in an occasional line, until the end of the scene. When this scene was over the rest of the cast was on stage so much that they couldn't leave the backstage area. I, on the other hand, had some time to myself. Being older, this was always a good time for me to take a bathroom break. On Friday night of the second weekend I had taken my break and was combing my hair in the makeup area when something in the mirror caught my eye. I saw a woman walking behind me in the tunnel. Because I was always the only one downstairs at this time, I turned to find out who had joined me. The woman was a complete stranger to me. She was costumed, if you can call it that, in a blouse with long, puffy sleeves. Her skirt was gathered at the waist and it belled out to the floor. I honestly don't remember if she wore a bonnet,

The downstairs hallway (the tunnel) where a spectral lady has been seen floating through walls.

but she did have some kind of head covering. She was no more than 25 feet away and turned sideways to me. I was amazed to see that she wasn't walking, but floating away from me across the floor. At this time I'm still wondering who this could be when she floated to, then through, the wall! Now she really had my attention! I took several steps into the tunnel when the hair on my neck and arms stood up and the goose bumps appeared. With no ghost hunting equipment and being all alone, I decided to rejoin the living. Up the stairs I shot, never missing a beat on stage. After the run of the show, and for several months afterwards, I interviewed many folks associated with the theater and found that a few other people have had an encounter with this woman. Before me, no one wanted to come forward for fear of being ridiculed. Boy, were they glad to have a sympathetic ear! The other three people who had seen the woman described her in great detail. She appeared exactly the same to all of us except for one major difference. Each of us saw her in a different color. One saw her in yellow. Another saw her in gray. One saw her in black, while I saw her in white. Now, as you may remember, I've always subscribed to the theory that if 10 people see the exact same car wreck, they'll have 10 different versions of that wreck. In this instance, all four of us described the exact same thing, just in a different color. I found this very odd. Maybe it was a mood ghost, I don't know.

While we're still downstairs, I'd like to describe two other areas of the theater that have drawn my attention. The work area of the makeup room constantly has people looking over their shoulders as if they caught a glimpse of something, or someone. At the entrance to the tunnel from the makeup/dressing rooms is the furnace closet. This rather large room contains several furnaces that heat the building. It is also a storage area for light bulbs, furnace filters, etc. Ernie and I are in this room more than anyone else. I always feel as if someone is standing right behind me here, as does Ernie. Nothing has been seen or heard, just that feeling.

At the end of the tunnel is the small prop area, which leads to the old bathrooms by the stairs that lead to the lobby on the main floor. The old bathrooms are gone now, but for years they were the topic of many a conversation. The bathrooms were used by the LGP when it first opened, but new facilities were quickly installed on the main level. When this happened, the old bathrooms were abandoned. The old toilet facilities were about six feet by five feet of very dark and water-rotted wood. This section of the basement often flooded until the theater bought and renovated the lot on the building's west side. Landscaping and new grass have halted the flow of rainwater. New plumbing has silenced the sewers. As cobwebs and dust enveloped the bathrooms, coupled with the dank smell of rotten wood, this abandoned monument to indoor plumbing gained a life of its own. Actors and other personnel described a dark and ominous feeling of someone lurking in the shadows in this lonely part of the basement. People seemed to scurry past the spot with blinders on to reach the stairway to the lobby. I, on many occasions, could only describe a feeling of sorrow and sadness in that area. Nothing was ever seen or heard.

The small staircase that leads to the front lobby has not been immune from otherworldly activity. One of the first major roles I had at the LGP was as the lecherous stage director, Lloyd Dallas, in the hilarious comedy, "Noises Off." If you've ever seen the movie, forget what you saw. The stage production is by far the best. At the beginning of the show I would make my entrance from the rear of the theater. During the opening music, so as not to be seen by late-arriving patrons, I would sit on the back basement steps until it was time for my entrance. Before every show I would whisper a little prayer asking God to just let me perform to the best of my ability, be that good or bad. As the adage goes, "There are no atheists in foxholes or on the stage." Before the last performance, which was a Sunday matinee, I was in my usual spot on the back stairs saying my prayer. I prayed a little harder before this show due to a hangover from the cast party the night before. As I sat in misery and solitude, I heard footsteps coming up the stairs towards me. I raised my aching head and opened my eyes puzzled at who could be invading my space. No one was there but the steps were still coming closer! Undaunted, or too hung over to care, I told whoever was there that I didn't have time for this; I had a show to do. As God is my witness, the footsteps stopped, and then went back down the stairs. I am fully aware that stairs creak in an old building, But on command? That was the beginning of my special connection with the old girl, the Looking Glass Playhouse.

Several years ago, the lobby, concession area and bathrooms were entirely renovated. For those of us in the paranormal world, the word "renovation" makes our ears perk up. Renovations of haunted areas seem to stir up all kinds of activity. As a concerned board member I would from time to time check the progress of the remodeling. Someone informed the workers that I was a ghost hunter. Before I knew it, large, hulking construction workers were babbling to me about weird things happening in the theater. Voices were heard, tools would move, shadows would fly across the walls, and workers would feel a tapping on their shoulders, as if someone were trying to get their attention. Of course, after turning around, no one would be there.

My favorite story of this period was when we needed some additional plumbing work done downstairs. I met the head plumber (no jokes, please!) one afternoon and escorted him into the basement to show him what work we needed done. The plumber was large man, at least six feet, five inches tall. He seemed to be very antsy and nervous the entire time we were downstairs. Finally he asked if we could go back upstairs because he needed something from his truck. When we got upstairs he took a deep breadth and began apologizing. He told me he just couldn't stand being in that basement any longer. He had heard about me and had planned to give me some good-natured kidding about ghosts but he never found the proper moment. He told me that the entire time we were downstairs, someone was tapping him on the left shoulder. When he would look to see who it was, it would stop. When he turned forward again, the tapping started back up. When the plumbing work was done at the theater, two different plumbers did the job.

Board members spend many hours in the front lobby. This is where the offices are located. Various members, though not seeing anything, report footsteps walking around on the second level. Occasionally, the sound of many people having a grand old time is heard in the theater.

Troy Taylor has often mentioned that places such as hospitals, churches, battlefields, and theaters, places that have been touched by much human activity and emotions over many years, can't help but leave some energy behind. More often than not, it's residual energy, just something left over. An intelligent haunting, something that interacts with the living, is very rare. When it came to the auditorium, I wasn't sure what I was dealing with. The auditorium has a series of rather large circular light bulbs along the walls on both sides that illuminate the theater. One of my jobs was to replace any burned-out bulbs. As you can imagine, we go through quite a few bulbs in the course of a year. On several occasions, while replacing bulbs, I've not only had the feeling of being watched, but I've also heard people talking. Sometimes it's a few, sometimes it's seemingly a crowd. On turning to see who has joined me, I always find that I'm quite alone. This has happened so often that I've come to expect it and I'm disappointed when it doesn't. I've set up tape recorders but have not been able to capture a voice other than mine.

All the seats in the theater are new. They are the kind that automatically fold up when they don't have a human butt holding them down. Once, while replacing a bulb, I heard a woman cough. On turning around I noticed that one of the seats was down. I mentioned out loud about it being a bad cough, then returned to the light bulb. When I was done and about to exit the theater, I saw that the seat was back up where it belonged. This episode has repeated itself on three other occasions.

Last, but certainly not least, is the stage itself. As mentioned earlier, the stage is not part of the original structure. It wasn't added till much later. That is what makes the strange occurrences that happen there so unusual. I've had lights come on as I've stumbled through the dark. I mentioned the earlier footsteps. Screw, nails, and even small tools, such as hammers and screwdrivers seem to appear from nowhere, when moments earlier they couldn't be found.

Now, before you think that I'm the only one having these strange experiences, I'd like to relate other tales of the paranormal that were told to me. My first show at the Looking Glass Playhouse introduced me to three individuals who have become some of my dearest friends. Linda Kaegal, Jenifer Elias, and Ernie Lingo took me under their collective wings and showed me the ropes at the theater. Because of their kindness and generosity, coupled with their warped and tainted sense of humor, we have developed a deep and lasting friendship. Ernie and Linda are a few years older than I, with Jenifer being the youngster, 17 years my junior. These three have been with the LGP for many, many years. Their theater tales run the gamut from the mundane to the otherworldly. Ernie and Linda have spent countless hours working on various theater projects. Their experiences echo mine, from the footsteps backstage to moving objects. They often describe hearing multiple voices in the auditorium, as if a crowd is in there. On inspection, an empty theater greets them.

Backstage at the Looking Glass Playhouse. Footsteps, whispers and mysterious helpers abound!

The stage is covered with various layers of huge, black curtains. When a scene is over and the lights are dimmed it is very hard to make your way to the back of the stage. On two occasions, Ernie has told me how the curtains actually parted to allow him access to the rear of the stage. On turning around to thank the helpful soul, no one was there. Ernie and Linda both told me about seeing someone up in the light booth. They saw him from the stage when the theater was shut down for various projects.

Jenifer is an entirely different story. She is short in stature, but long on energy. She is one of the theater gnomes. A theater gnome is an individual who is at the playhouse at all hours of the day and night, delivering supplies or working on repairing whatever disaster has befallen the building. Now Jen is at the theater the same times as the rest of us, but she has reported no unusual activity, or at least none that she can't explain. I believe that because she is always in such a hurry because of her many jobs and other obligations, that she doesn't have time to experience anything. She is literally rushing in and out with the blinders on.

Unfortunately, several occurrences have happened to change our little group of friends. Jenifer has relocated to Branson, Mo., because of work. Ernie can't afford to come to the theater as often because of the high price of gasoline. Last of all, and the most painful, is that Linda passed away about a year and a half ago. It was very sudden and completely unexpected. The shock has passed, but not our feeling of loss.

These are just a few of the many stories related to me, and experienced by me. I'm bombarded on a weekly basis by fellow thespians and assorted workers looking for answers to the strange happenings at the Looking Glass Theater. My gut feeling is that the playhouse is a happy setting for both the living and the non-living. With Scott Air Force Base dominating the area, many people find friendships and an outlet for their talents in Lebanon. This happy place has brought pleasure to thousands over the years. For some folks whom I know of, this was their only time of happiness. If spirits can be in transition, and I've come to believe that they can, then a quick stop at their happy place doesn't seem so far-fetched. The many years of renovations have stirred up and changed the activity, but again, it has always been positive.

I know that not everyone believes in the paranormal. And remember, something is only paranormal until it is explained. Then it becomes part of the normal. My views on ghosts and their activities at the Looking Glass Playhouse are not shared by all of the board members. The Looking Glass Playhouse is a community theater, open to all. Free speech and thought are encouraged every year by the body of work that is put out by the theater. If you don't believe in ghosts and their activities at the theater, I support you 100 percent. I just ask that you keep an open mind on the subject. And who knows? Maybe some night when the fellow patron seated next to you won't respond to your attempts at a conversation, it may be because he or she is there for a different reason. Maybe they're just passing through.

The Board of Directors of the Looking Glass Playhouse has graciously given me permission to write about my impressions of the grand old place. These are my views. They are neither endorsed nor suppressed by the board. I thank them for their understanding and assistance in letting me write about the place I love so much.

The Looking Glass Playhouse light booth, where a mysterious man makes frequent appearances

NO GHOSTS BEHIND THE COUNTER

It always amazes me how our sense of smell can transport us through time. During Christmas, Kim turns our house into a heaven of confectionary delights. Who among us has smelled the aroma of fresh-baked sugar cookies and not recalled being a child in our mother's kitchen? Who can smell fresh pine trees and not be reminded of Christmas?

For a journey through the past you need only travel to Legendary Creations Candle & Gift Shop at 206 W. Saint Louis St. Janet and Rick Schmitt have owned the shop since 2002. Janet worked for the Symer family who were the original owners. When the opportunity arose for her to own it herself, Janet couldn't resist.

Over the years, Janet has become one of my best friends and favorite people in Lebanon. Rick is a big guy with a big heart and sense of humor to match.

Among my favorite merchandise in Janet's store is her collection of Yankee Candles. These jars of aromatic gold are what keep me coming back again and again. Well, those and the hauntings. Kim and I have visited the store on many of our day trips to Lebanon. The call of the candles is too seductive to resist. Janet also has many seasonal treasures. Our favorites are Santa Claus figurines. Kim is a collector and I of course can't say no to her.

Janet was already a friend by the summer of 2003, when my walking regimen kept me parading up and down the streets of Lebanon. Janet knew about my interest in the paranormal but hesitated to share her experiences in the gift store. Finally, the unexplainable happenings could be ignored no longer. Janet phoned and asked me to come to the store as soon as I could.

One bright and cheery afternoon (see, it doesn't always have to be a dark and stormy night) I strolled into Legendary Creations with paper and pen in hand. Of course, being the good ghost hunter that I am, I was also armed with a camera and a tape recorder. For an hour I sat in the back room with Janet and Donna, one of Janet's longtime employees. It

Legendary Creations

wasn't long before I had amassed quite a catalogue of strange happenings. The unexplainable occurrence that had happened in that very room, not more than two hours before is what caused Janet to ask for my help.

The back room is where Janet prices new merchandise, marks the sale items and fixes broken racks and displays. Earlier in the day, when Janet and Donna were having lunch, they watched in astonishment as a cardboard box started to dance across a long countertop. The box was about a foot square and was empty, except for some compressed foam packing. Donna said the box just suddenly started to bounce around on its corners as it made its way along the counter. When the dance of the magical box had ceased, Janet went over and promptly knocked it onto the floor. Once they were certain the cardboard cube was dead, they picked it up and examined it carefully inside and out. Other than the packing material there was nothing inside. Their first thought was that a mouse had gotten into the box. There was no mouse, and there wasn't likely to be one since the store is kept very clean. I examined the counter for a possible wind source, but there was none. There was a fan about 10 feet away so I placed the box on the counter and turned the fan on to its highest setting. Nothing moved.

This was not the first unexplainable event in the store. My notes were a testament to that. Through the doorway behind the back room are twin landings with steps going up to a storage area and down to the bathroom and basement. The stairs are a high area of energy. Footsteps are often heard ascending and descending at all hours of the day and night. The footsteps sound like they are being made by someone wearing hard-soled shoes. Everybody who works in the store wears tennis shoes.

The main aisle at Legendary Creations, where many have had encounters with ghostly footsteps, including my wife, Kim

The front door of the establishment is a wooden frame with a large glass insert. The door is the original from 1918 and is very heavy and solid. Often, before the store is open for business, the door is heard to open and close, along with the sound of the brass bells that are grazed each time the door is opened to announce the arrival of a customer. Footsteps walk towards the register in the rear of the store. Whoever is working on these mornings is usually frightened, as the store hasn't been opened for business yet. On examination, the front door is found to be closed and the dead bolt fastened. There is no one is in sight. The arrival of the first real customer of the day after the shop opens at 10 a.m. is always a welcome relief.

Over the years I have found that instead of choosing to bother someone at random, entities are more likely to be attracted to a person who gives out a certain kind of energy. This seems to be the case at Legendary Creations, where Sarah Ruth is a young and vibrant employee. Sarah knew me from the Alton Haunting Tours a full year before we became reacquainted in Lebanon. I feel that Sarah's sunny disposition is what makes her a target for the odd goings-on in the store; it's like a lighted candle attracting a moth.

The front door episodes have happened often when Sarah has been working in the store, as well as the parade of footsteps. Even though she doesn't like them, she has accepted the strange happenings as part of the job.

The building that houses Legendary Creations is the second structure to occupy 206 W. Saint Louis St. The original burned down in a sensational fire on

August 5, 1917. Four businesses were destroyed in the blaze, with 206 housing the C.H. Sager Hardware Co. The other buildings that burned were the H.W. Blanck Mercantile Company, Stoffel Brothers Hardware Company and the Ben Bunge Bakery. The fire was believed to have started in a pile of oily rags in the basement of the hardware store where Legendary Creations stands today. Something good came out of the ashes of the fire in 1917: the townspeople of Lebanon realized that they were in need of a proper fire department with updated equipment Since that time, the Lebanon Fire Department takes a backseat to no one for response time and firefighting capabilities.

In 1946, a couple by the name of Emil and Odelia Weber purchased the building. For three generations the E & R Weber Hardware Store operated at 206 W. Saint Louis St.

Legendary Creations moved to that site in 1993, when Jon and Susan Symer bought the place. Their original shop was down the street at 120 W. Saint Louis St., where the St. Louis Street Cafe is today. Customers can still walk the old wooden floors and see the original tin ceiling from 1918."

This has been another frustrating location to try to match up the historical events and personages to the hauntings of today. I'm sure that residual energy abounds throughout the building. I also believe that Janet and Sarah are the flames that ignite many of the episodes.

The night we investigated the location, my team consisted of myself, my wife, Kim, Luke Naliborski and Bill Alsing. We met Rick Schmitt about 8 p.m. on a crisp winter evening. Rick takes the strange goings-on in his store in stride and usually leaves me to my own devices. After a tour of the premises, Rick locked us in and promised to return about midnight. Just to do things a little differently, I gave the team the full history of the site. After discussing the stories and seeing the locations, we planned out our vigil sites. I, of course, would get the basement. Luke went to the upstairs storage area. This was a welcome departure for Luke; normally we stuff him up into a nasty cramped attic. This time he'd have an entire level where he could walk around easily. Kim took the front sales floor and Bill was left to roam at will. Bill just has a sense about where to wander and where to avoid. He comes up with great photos by working his way.

The basement, although a little dusty, wasn't too bad a place to spend time. The foundation is made up of a concrete floor and brick walls. While walking past a pile of small pieces of lumber, I got hit in the back of the head by a chunk of brick. Even though it hurt, it was exciting! Over the years of investigations I have been hit, slapped, scratched, had my hair pulled and been knocked down. A small piece of brick was nothing. I turned on all the basement lights and examined the room where I stood. The thrill of the flying brick rapidly faded. I found that as I was walking past the pile of lumber I had stepped on the end of a two by four. The board had the piece of brick on the end. As I stepped down on one end of the board, the piece of brick flew up as if propelled by a catapult and that's why it hit me from behind. Another mystery solved.

As I mentioned earlier, the back staircase with the twin landings has seen more than its share of supernatural activity. My favorite story was when Sarah was sitting on a step just above the second landing. She was chatting away with Janet downstairs. Sarah turned as she heard the second floor storage area door open and close. Then the hard-soled shoe footsteps came down the stairs and right past where Sarah was seated. They made it to the bottom step, then stopped. Sarah told me she could actually feel the steps vibrate as the footfalls moved past her. Janet heard them also. To our disappointment, on the night of our vigil we were unable to capture anything on film or on our tape recorders.

Bill had made his way to the second floor with Luke. I was still in the basement, which left Kim by herself on the main level.

When I talk about our energies being attractive to entities I use the moth to a flame example. Some folks' flames seem to burn higher and brighter than others. Kim's is a campfire. By leaving her alone on the first floor, we were out of range if she required any assistance.

By 11 p.m., the only illumination in the main level of the store was from the streetlight outside. The light came from across the street and through the two picture windows and the glass in the front door. It was something, but not much.

Kim, with camera in hand, wanders into areas where she feels electricity in the air. She also has the good sense to know when something isn't right and it's time to scoot. As she was standing in the darkened area by the cash register, she heard the front door open and close. The little bell that announces a customer even tinkled a bit. If Kim knew what was coming next she would've tinkled a bit herself! While focusing her eyes on the dimly lit front door, Kim

The back staircase where Sarah heard footsteps and felt the vibration of the steps as someone passed her.

heard footsteps coming toward her. The hard-soled steps approached at a casual pace. The only thing upsetting about these footfalls was that no one was attached to them. As the invisible but audible steps drew nearer, Kim called out for us. Sadly for her, we were out of earshot. The footsteps didn't stop until they were within two feet of Kim. She said later that the air around her felt freezing cold at this point. As I lounged about in the basement, my spider sense started to tingle. I had a feeling I should go upstairs. I met Kim in the back room. The expression on her face told me all that I needed to know. Something had happened!

Just as Kim had finished filling me in on all the details of her encounter, Bill and Luke suddenly appeared. We entered the sales floor En masse. By now, there was nothing to see or hear. Kim had evidently been yelling for us to assist her in her time of need. I don't recall hearing a thing. Bill and Luke were going over some video footage. We may have caught some movement upstairs. It's nothing earth shattering, so it goes in our "maybe" file. We decided to try and recreate the events that Kim had described. The door was still locked and bolted. It could not have moved the bells. We checked for any air currents that may have moved them. Again, nothing. The footsteps were strike three; we all were wearing tennis shoes and Kim heard hard-soled shoes. I have been in the store on many occasions since that night. Even with traffic moving on the main street out front, the building is solid. No vehicle, no matter how big and lumbering, can cause a vibration that would create strange sounds in the shop. We did record fluctuating temperature readings throughout the night.

Our night was rapidly coming to a close, but not without one more fright. We gathered up our gear and reassembled to pack up. It suddenly got dark. The light from outside was almost gone. As we gazed at the front door, a massive shadow of a man stood in the doorway.

Quietly, the figure moved toward us. We all turned our flashlights on the dark figure at the same moment. To our intense relief, the shadowy figure was Rick Schmitt. The time had flown by so quickly that we didn't realize it was now midnight. Rick said he came in as quietly as he could because he didn't know if were filming or not. Breathing a sigh of relief, we bid him goodnight.

Our spirits sank during our review of our film footage and tape recordings because nothing concrete was captured. There were a few interesting moments, but nothing definite to report. Our only oddities came from the temperature drops in the main area.

Eyewitness accounts are another matter altogether. Sarah was badly frightened one afternoon as a full figure apparition of a woman walked from a side room into the back room. When this happened the figure was no more than 10 feet away from Sarah. A check of the back room turned up nothing.

On a recent Sunday morning, before the store was open for business, Sarah and Janet heard footsteps run up to the storeroom and then race up and down the aisle on the sales floor for a full minute.

While in the office, Janet has the footsteps on the staircase as a constant companion.

Recently, while leaving the upstairs storeroom with an armful of merchandise, Janet berated herself aloud for not turning on the lights. Almost immediately the lights sprang to life. Janet was alone. Or so she thought.

The spot in front of the cash register where Kim had her eerie experience is prone to abrupt temperature variances. Twenty-degree temperature drops are not uncommon. Next to this area is where a figure is occasionally spotted out of the corner of one's eye. Turning around to check on the would-be customer reveals no one is there.

I have sat down with Janet and the crew on many occasions and gone over the timeline of events at the store. Although we believe that quite a bit of the activity is residual, there seems to be something more going on. Because of the closeness of the activity to Janet and Sarah, we have come to suspect that a deceased family member may be involved. Because we haven't pegged who exactly is there, we won't put anything on paper yet. We are rapidly narrowing down the list. We also believe a male presence to be at the location. With so many suspects to choose from, we won't even try to venture a guess at this time.

Just remember that the tale doesn't end because a story has been written. All of the tales in Lebanon are works in progress. This book is just part one.

So, come to Legendary Creations, buy a candle, buy a gift and peek into the past!

An area of Legendary Creations where mysterious patrons appear and disappear

STAND STILL
I'M TRYING TO COOK

During my numerous investigations I have realized that there are no hard and fast rules as to why a location becomes haunted. I have found no experts in this field. There are individuals whose opinions I respect greatly. Friends such as Troy Taylor, Rosemary Ellen Guiley and John Zaffis have helped guide me along the way. I respect their integrity, research methods, and experiences but I don't always agree with them. That's the beauty of an organization such as The American Ghost Society: we are free to form our own opinions. We share and discuss our research and findings, but we are individuals who can disagree.

I have found that the age of a place has nothing to do with whether it becomes haunted or not. Also, it doesn't matter if one person or many have occupied a site; it's the events that happen there leave an impression. To sum up, when it comes to set rules down in stone, there truly are none. This doesn't mean that we don't have a set of procedures that we all follow. Legitimate paranormal researchers are very respectful of locations. We're like vampires: we don't come in unless invited. We are also respectful of individuals, whether dead or alive.

Careful research by Lebanon resident Jo Turk led her to contact me about a possible haunting at her restaurant, the St. Louis Street Café, 120 W. Saint Louis St. The building that houses the restaurant has been around since before the turn of turn of the 20th fcentury.

In 1875, Christian Haenel and Julius Hoffmann, Jr., bought the lot that houses today's restaurant and the lot to the east of it, which is a city park today. The twin lots cost $2,050 at the time.

On the lot that today contains the city park, Julius Hoffmann, Jr., built a cigar factory. It was one of three such factories in town. The other cigar makers were the Brown Brothers (today this is a chiropractic office), and Henry Traband's cigar shop which today is the Town 'N Country Gift Shop.

In 1907, Christian Haenel's widow sold the west lot for $3,200 to William Buhr, who turned the building into a shoe store. He rented the upstairs to Charles and Anne Marie Frey, who not only lived there, but also operated a Prudential Insurance office.

In 1927, for the grand total of $48 a month, The Kroger Grocery and Baking Company

Hoffman Cigar Factory and House. It was later torn down to make way for a park (below)

ran a store on the lower level. The building continued to change hands as Marion and Jeanette Grupe bought it in 1941. It was now an insurance office downstairs with Marion Grupe's law office on the second floor.

The next owners didn't arrive until 1969, when Lloyd and Ruby Jones purchased the building, followed by John and Bonnie Wright in 1977, who promptly leased it out. It was now the Shepherd's Inn. John and Dona Schieppe bought the place from the Wrights and opened their own restaurant, "Schiappa's." At this time, Legendary Creations Candle & Gift Shop was opened and operated upstairs for two years before moving to its current address.

Kurt and Mary Beth Anheuser bought the property in 1992. The Anheusers ran the Heritage Brass Bed Company in the rear of the building. In the front section, a lady named Betty Close ran a store called Close to Nature. In 1995 Betty moved her business down the street and the Anheusers renovated the front half of the building and opened the St. Louis Street Cafe.

On the east lot, the Hoffmann Cigar Factory stood for many years. When it went out of business it remained a residence for Julius Hoffman's daughter, Frieda, who lived there until the day she died.

St. Louis Street Café

The Lebanon Beautification Committee bought the property and turned it into a park. About five years ago, the park was donated to the city of Lebanon.

In June of 1998, Jo and Walt Turk bought 120 W. Saint Louis St. They kept the name and took over the operation of the St. Louis Street Cafe. Their daughter, Kathi Turk, became co-manager and lived upstairs for a year with her son.

It was Jo and Kathi who decided to take a chance on me and see if I could explain the weird events that were unfolding on a daily basis at the restaurant.

In March of 2003, I sat down at the restaurant with them and recorded their tales of the unexplained.

From May of 2001 through May of 2002, Kathi lived upstairs with her 16-year-old son. They both would hear footsteps move from the foyer through each room and then stop back in the foyer. The footsteps sounded like hard-soled shoes on the wooden floor. Kathi said they could hear the distinct sound of heel-toe, heel-toe, as the footsteps circled.

Throughout the upper level, the sound of a large, heavy door being slammed was heard. All the doors upstairs are lightweight interior doors or accordion doors. None of them could make the loud sound that had been heard. The front door to the apartment is barely audible when it is slammed. The loudest sound when the front door is slammed is made by the jangling of the little bell on the door. The bell was never heard during the occurrences. Kathi said the door sounds stopped on a regular basis after about three months.

Kathi's bedroom presented its own problems. Boy, that sounded bad! Read on and I'll try to dig myself out of this hole. When Kathi would sit at her makeup table on the far wall, she would be overwhelmed by the smell of bubblegum. She described the scent as if someone chewed a fresh piece of gum for several seconds, then breathed in her face. The only way to make it stop was to leave the room. Items in the bedroom would disappear and reappear in the strangest places. Kathi's pink slippers seemed to be a constant target. The fuzzy footies would just vanish. Kathi would find them days later in such places as a windowsill, on top of doorways, etc. Thought frustrating, it was far from threatening.

The upstairs activity doesn't have a set pattern. It seems to intensify during renovations. At those times, it seems more things are stirred up than paint.

At the time, Kathi owned a very old cat that wasn't afraid of anyone or anything. The ancient feline would make its way to the living room and stare into the corner for up to 20 minutes at a time. It was as if someone was standing there, holding the cat's attention. To stop this from happening, Kathi put her fish tank in the offending corner. The cat would just stare beyond the tank.

The lights had a life of their own, they would go on and off at will. The wiring and switches were old, but they passed every test the electricians gave them.

At the time of my initial interview a tenant by the name of Ami Payne was living upstairs. Ami worked for Jo Turk in the café and shared the apartment with a roommate. I questioned Ami separately from Jo and Kathi. She related many of the same experiences that Kathi had told me. Ami and her roommate also heard the footsteps parade through the foyer. They also experienced the feeling of being watched. Small items were still disappearing and reappearing. What really grabbed my attention was when Ami talked about smelling bubblegum in one of the bedrooms.

Lest you believe that the second floor was the only area of activity, we'll now detail the happenings on the ground floor.

Jo, Kathi and Ami all verified this tale. It seems that almost everyone who has worked in the cafe has heard his or her name called. The voice comes from the area between the kitchen and the cash register. Whenever someone turns around to see who is calling, there is never anybody there.

One many a morning, whoever opens for the day finds the chairs pulled out from the tables. They appear as if someone where sitting in them. All the tables and chairs in the cafe have been involved at one time or another. Crumbs are also found on the table as if someone had been eating there. Jo and Kathi are now friends of mine. I know for a fact that cafe would've been spotless when they left for the day.

Throughout the entire building people have felt a light touch on their arms or backs, as if someone is brushing a hand against them.

Workers in the kitchen report feeling watched. The sensation is especially intense in the dishwasher area.

The event that shattered Kathi's courage happened in the basement. The basement houses the ice machine, freezers, storage closets and the cafe office. Early mornings would find Kathi in the office, preparing for the day. Often she felt as if she were not alone. Footsteps would start at the top of the concrete steps, go down the steps, walk through the basement and stop at the doorway to the office. I know it's hard to believe, but you can actually get used to something like this. If it happens often enough it just becomes part of the daily ritual. But that can change in an instant.

One bright and sunny morning, Kathi was in the office when the footsteps began. This time something was different. The air felt heavier and charged with electricity. As the footfalls drew nearer the door, the doorway seemed to fill up with a presence. Kathi described it like looking through a screen door.

Doorway to the former office in the basement of the St. Louis Street Café. Cold spots, a hazy mist and a force that seemed to be able to bend a door over the threshold were encountered here.

This morning, when the footsteps stopped, the show wasn't over. As the temperature in the room started to fall, Kathi's attention was drawn to the wooden threshold of the doorway. It started to creak and bend as if a great weight were resting on it. To see the threshold bend was extraordinary because while it is only a little over and inch in thickness, the threshold rests on eight inches of brick. It had nowhere to bend, and yet it did! Kathi doesn't remember how long this went on. Eventually the threshold straightened out and the phantom screen door disappeared....and so did Kathi!

After explaining to her mother what had happened, Kathi realized that she had a dilemma. There was no other location for the office. That's when Kathi's philosophy changed. She told herself that if she didn't see anything, then nothing was happening. She marched downstairs and turned her desk around. With her back to the door, she would now be oblivious to any unnatural force.

The stories I collected that day were wonderful. It's easy to not be afraid when you're not involved. There was one last story, and yes, I was involved.

As I've mentioned on numerous occasions, the Looking Glass Playhouse Community Theater puts on a walking ghost story tour through the streets of Lebanon. Every October, patrons are entertained by costumed thespians telling classic tales of horror. Before I started telling real ghost stories in Alton, I was a part of Haunted Happenings in Lebanon.

The path that our patrons walk brings them to the city park, east of the St. Louis Street Cafe. After the ghost story from the gazebo, they parade past the cafe to their next destination. It was 1999 or 2000 that a strange connection between the Haunted Happenings crowds and the St. Louis Street Cafe was made. Several times over the weekend, as a tour group was passing the cafe, etched-glass mugs would shatter for no apparent reason. They started shattering in the back by the dishwasher. Then glasses shattered on the front counter and finally glasses were exploding in the front window. The front window episode happened right in the presence of a tour group. The well-made glasses were quite heavy and not prone to break. I was involved with Haunted Happenings that night. It was the first of many odd tales that I heard about the place.

Before I could launch a formal investigation of the St. Louis Street Cafe, Jo put it up for sale. It was on the market less than a week. I was excited that new owners were taking over, but afraid that they wouldn't warm up to the cold spots. My fears were unjustified.

Kathy and Heberts reopened the restaurant under its former name. Kathy had been warned about me by Jo Turk and my arrival was expected. Even though Kathy didn't believe in the hauntings, she did allow me free reign of the place.

Again, I picked a weeknight for the investigation because I felt it would be quieter. The team that night would be Bill Alsing and his friend Wendy, who was on loan from another paranormal investigation group. We would not have access to the second floor as three women from Scott Air Force Base had moved into the apartment. Kathy promised to let me know if they encountered anything unusual. I didn't want to prejudice them, one way or the other.

Arriving about 30 minutes before Bill and Wendy, I decided to enter the cafe and start to set up some of the equipment. This was my first time alone there. The lights being dimmed didn't help calm me either. I heard sounds coming from the basement. The source of the sounds eventually revealed themselves to be the ice machine, the furnace and two large freezers.

As I reentered the front of the cafe after my trip to the basement, I must have jumped a foot as two shadowy figures loomed in the doorway. The figures revealed themselves to be Bill and Wendy. They were peering through the front door in hopes of attracting my attention. I had locked myself in and them out. After gathering what dignity I had left, I opened the door.

As I mentioned earlier, Bill Alsing is an officer of the American Ghost Society and owner of the History & Hauntings Bookstore in Alton. Bill is a vital part of my paranormal research group, PRIME, which stands for Paranormal Research In the Metro-East. I wish I could take credit for that name, but it was Luke Naliborski's brainchild. I had met Wendy several times before.

After our initial hellos, I walked Wendy and Bill through the building. I only gave them small details, as I wanted them to form their own opinions. Nothing came readily available to either of them. I decided to fill them in on the location's strange happenings.

It was now time to split up. Because the main level is so large, Bill and Wendy would stay up there and I would go to my normal spot in the basement. Bidding my partners in crime goodbye, I proceeded to the lower regions and to Kathi Turk's former office, which was now a storage area. Unfazed, I set up my camera equipment across the hall and aimed it at the former office doorway. I then took a chair and parked my caboose just inside the storage area. The only light I could see was the red dot from the infrared light on my video camera. In the darkness one minute led to two. Two minutes led to three...three minutes led to sixty. Oh my God! I had fallen asleep!! I warned you that ghost hunting wasn't always exciting. The phantom screen door could have slammed in my face and I would've slept right through.

As I was pondering on how to explain to the others why I hadn't noticed anything, Bill came downstairs. He was worried because I am not usually so quiet. More often than not, you can locate me in the darkness by the sound of a potato chip bag opening or a soda can popping open. I lied to Bill and told him not a thing was going on in the basement. Bill let me know that Wendy was getting some readings on the TriField Meter. Wherever she went, the readings followed. So there we were: Wendy upstairs with possible activity and Bill and I downstairs talking about possible activity. Before we decided what to do next, Wendy entered the basement, TriField Meter in tow. I didn't believe that the meters were of any use in basements. Heavy wiring and multiple appliances would give off a multitude of false readings.

So there we were, the three of us in the darkened basement. After noticing a small temperature drop, I went behind my video camera and waited. Three small balls of white light appeared. The balls shot up and down the ceiling. Wherever they went, they never ventured far from Wendy. After reviewing the film, I don't know what they were. The jury is still out.

We decided to call it a night and gathered up our equipment. On further review, nothing worth mentioning came from our visit. But the stories keep on coming.

After a couple of years, the airbase ladies moved out of the upstairs apartment and an acquaintance of mine moved in. Over the years, young, talented actresses have played the role of a Fezziwig daughter in the Looking Glass Playhouse production of "A Christmas Carol." I, as Mr. Fezziwig, have watched these girls mature into young ladies. One of my favorite "daughters" was Carrie McNeil. Carrie is now living upstairs at the St. Louis Street Cafe. When not attending college classes, she also works in the cafe.

Carrie and her brother, who shares the apartment, have witnessed many strange happenings of their own. The footsteps are back. The feeling of being watched is back. Now there is a new twist: both Carrie and her brother have experienced the sensation of someone sitting on the edge of their beds. Those who have had that experience know it can be quite unsettling.

Carrie is also a target in the cafe as well as Jessica, who does the cooking on many occasions. Trips to the basement are carefully planned and executed in a hurry. Those who dawdle find themselves confronted with cups or napkins flying off the shelves. A feeling of not being alone is quite prevalent in the basement.

As Carrie's school schedule has increased her time in the cafe has decreased. With the time in the cafe having lessened, the chance of paranormal encounters has dwindled. That is a good thing for Carrie.

Now Jessica became the focal point of ghostly fixations. Jessica's invisible visitor appears at the most inopportune times. While preparing lunches at a breakneck pace, she is often startled by the figure of a man standing in the side room. On investigation, no one is ever found. One afternoon, the spectral figure appeared three times in the span of three minutes. To hold the apparition at bay, Jessica rolled a metal serving trolley into the doorway. The trolley must have helped because he never showed for the rest of the day. I probably shouldn't refer to him as a spectral figure. When he appears, he is as solid-looking as anyone you'll meet on the street. I happened to see him during my initial interview with Jo and Kathie Turk. As I was setting up, I spied a man walking through the back area. When I mentioned to Jo that I thought there only the three of us, she grew pale. I had just seen one of the ghosts she needed to tell me about! The man is often glimpsed out of the corner of one's eye. Most of the time he is complete. At other times he is only partially visible.

During a Haunted Lebanon tour last October, we were in the St. Louis Street Cafe. The group was too large to get everyone in the basement at the same time. Realizing that half the crowd were smokers, I took them downstairs first. After that part of the story was completed, I let them outside to puff away. Then I locked the door! Making sure I had everyone, we made our way to the basement. I arranged everyone toward the back of the basement by the former office. The only light came from the top of the staircase. As I was telling the stories of unexplained happenings in the basement, my eyes caught sight of someone standing at the top of the stairs. The figure wore dark brownish pants and boots of some kind. I was angry at first because I thought someone from the group of smokers had gotten back into the building. Then I was puzzled as to how they had accomplished that feat. Never breaking stride with my stories, I made my way to the bottom of the steps. Just as the legs were turning away, I peered up the steps to see just that. A pair of legs! There were legs from just below the knee through the feet, but there was no body attached. I never stopped once during my stories. If I panic, the group will panic.

On turning around, I was stopped by a young girl's screams. She wasn't screaming at the ghostly figure, she was screaming at me. "What did you see?" she demanded. I replied that I hadn't seen a thing. She accused of me lying. Since the rest of the group also demanded to know, I told them what I saw at the top of the stairs. We left the basement as one solid hunk of humanity.

Chairs moving, objects flying, and a ghostly figure in brown are daily staples at the St. Louis Street Cafe. Come on in and have a wonderful lunch. And, who knows...maybe the girls can scare up something for dessert.

The basement steps at the St. Louis Street Café where the author encountered a pair of disembodied legs during a Haunted Lebanon Tour.

The St. Louis Street Café front dining area.

I'M NOT MOVING THAT

Back in October of 2003, I was featured in the *Belleville News Democrat* newspaper. The Sunday magazine was featuring stories about Halloween. The article written by reporter Jaime Ingle, turned out quite nicely.

One of the locations we visited was the Bittersweet Gift and Antique Shop located at 121 W. St. Louis St. A friend of mine, Lynette Rehkop, owned and operated the shop. Lynette was one of the first people in Lebanon to come to me with a ghostly tale.

You can only imagine how hectic it is when you set a time for your grand opening and you realize that you are falling way behind. Only days from her opening, Lynette was running around like a woman possessed. She soon found herself working late into the night.

The store itself was very narrow, with long walls. The evening in question turned out to be a one-person painting party. By midnight one of the long side walls was completed. Not only were the walls long, they were about 10 feet high. Five feet from the now freshly painted wall stood a massive cabinet. The cabinet was almost as tall as the ceiling and over 20 feet long. Lynette, alone and exhausted, decided that she wanted the cabinet in its place against the wall. Her husband and his friends were gong to show up the next day to move the behemoth but that didn't matter to Lynette. She wanted it moved right away. Throwing reason to the wind, she grabbed the end of the cabinet and tugged. Within seconds, she realized it wasn't going anywhere. Then Lynette did what any of us would've done: she started cussing at the cabinet. Suddenly, as her hands still rested on it, the huge cabinet slid from five feet away right up to the wall! Not knowing whether to scream or pass out, Lynette grabbed her purse and left for the night.

The next morning during breakfast, Lynette tried to tell her husband that he and his friends didn't need to go to the store to move the cabinet. She said that she had taken care of it. Of course, her husband didn't believe her and showed up with friends in tow about an hour later. To their amazement, the large cabinet was right where Lynette had told them. The men couldn't explain how she moved it, but their backs were safe for another day.

The next night, Lynette was again alone at the shop and burning the midnight oil. By midnight, she had finished painting the opposite wall. Thankfully, there wasn't a cabinet to move. As Lynette was sealing up the paint can, she was hit with the heavy aroma of a burning cigar. Lynette

Tivoli Antique Store (Formerly Bittersweet Antiques & Gifts)

is as anti-smoking as one can get. She yelled out to the offending presence, "This is my store and I don't allow smoking of any kind!" The venomous vapors disappeared! This time her feelings weren't ones of fear, but accomplishment.

Since that time, I have tape recorded and photographed every square inch of the store. My efforts have produced no results.

Lynette also spoke of feeling frightened when she went into the basement. It became so bad that she eventually refused to go down there at all. The foundation does sit right up against the foundation of the Tapestry Room Restaurant. Maybe it's guilt by association.

Historically, the location at 121 W. Saint Louis St. has a varied past. The property was originally sold to William Welsch in 1827. Welsch bought the property from Thomas Ray. The structure that sits there now wasn't constructed until 1878.

Charles and Annie Frey ran a bakery there between 1921 through 1947. It was a blessing for Charles that the upstairs section of the building was rather large. He and Annie had four children. That made six people in total occupying the space. After Annie died, Charles married Carrie Peachy. Carrie had four children. Our living body count is now 10. Charles and Carrie had two additional children for a grand sum of 12 people living upstairs.

Before the Freys bought the place, around 1920, it housed the first bowling alley in Lebanon. The east side of the building was a candy and soda store called the Rest-A-While. The two-lane bowling alley was in the back. Johnny Jacobs owned the Rest-A-While. Jacobs was either very lazy or a genius. To speed up the cleaning of the oak floors every night, he drilled holes all over the floor. By doing this when he slopped the water around to clean at the end of the day, it drained through the holes and into the dirt-floored basement below. Dave's Pool Hall also operated at the site, as well as Grandma's Attic, an antique shop owned by Joe and Ann Zimmerlee.

The history of the site didn't seem relevant to the hauntings. Further research did reveal that the large cabinet that gave Lynette such a hard time was originally in the chemistry lab at McKendree College. But I could find no reason for a spirit to attach itself to the piece of furniture.

Lynette has since moved out and the Tivoli Antique Shop has been operating there for the last two years. The new owner knew of my work and promised to let me know if anything unexplainable happened. The inside of the store has been totally renovated. The moving cabinet has been banished to the basement.

This location is now a part of the Haunted Lebanon Tours that I do for fun and exercise. During a tour last year, I was telling the story about the cigar smoke when a woman from the back of the crowd yelled that she knew the identity of the ghost. According to her, it was her grandfather, a gentleman by the name of Art Webb. On second thought it may have been her uncle. I'm not sure. I wasn't able to write down the information for an hour or more. Webb lived in the back of the building and was a notorious cigar smoker. I got the impression he was a lot like Kramer on "Seinfeld." Webb was described as very friendly. He would spend his days visiting with acquaintances all over town. Art Webb died in 1966. I'm not saying he is the smoking ghost, but he sure fits the bill.

As of this writing, the Tivoli Antique Shop is a busy place. Busy with the living. No cigar smoke or moving objects have been reported. Renovations can stir up activity, but they can also quiet a location. Although the place has calmed down, for me, there's always hope of a relapse.

THE LEGEND OF
RHODA

There are many people who believe that an encounter with the paranormal is the equivalent of coming face to face with a demon. I'm not saying these folks are wrong, but there are varying viewpoints on the subject.

Every major religion in the world believes in an afterlife. Every major religion believes that the body dies but the soul lives on. This soul, or life force is what remains.

I'm just questioning some of the interpretations of what happens to us when we die. Maybe it's not all cut and dried like we've been taught. I questioned everything as a child and have continued to do so to this day. What if a person physically dies but things don't progress the way we all presume that they should? What happens if you don't immediately go to heaven or hell or wherever you're suppose to go at that point? What if your soul stays earthbound for whatever reason? If someone with a living physical body encounters you, they are not dealing with a demon, but just with you. If a person's spirit is indeed that person, it logically follows that their state of mind is still the same. If you are nice in life, it should follow that you will be nice in the afterlife. If you're a jerk in life, again, you would be the same in the afterlife.

During countless paranormal investigations, I've encountered many wonderful souls on the other side. I've also met some real jerks. Though the energy was negative, it wasn't harmful. And then came Rhoda.

One bright summer day in 2003, I received a call from a young lady names Britany Robichau. Britany is the daughter of a friend from the Looking Glass

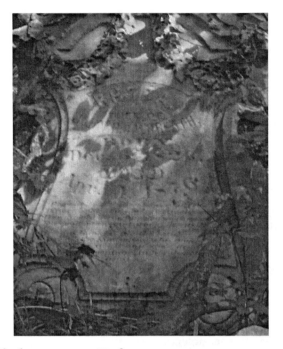

Rhoda's gravestone was found in a wooded area near a cornfield -- an impossible place to find without out guides.

(Left) A close-up of Rhoda's gravestone, giving at least a basis in truth to the story that had been told about her by generations of Lebanon teenagers.

(Below) A view of the small cemetery in the woods. Rhoda's stone is shown propped up in the center.

Playhouse, Cindy Robichau. It seems that Britany was telling Cindy of a local haunting that she and some friends had heard about. Cindy, knowing my interest in the paranormal, had Britany contact me immediately.

I met Britany the next day in Lebanon. She was 18 years old at the time and a student at Southwestern Illinois College. She regaled me with a tale of murder and revenge at a small cemetery hidden in the woods. The version I got was that a woman named Rhoda was mad at her husband when he left to fight in the Civil War. Either due to his leaving or perhaps insanity, she killed all 13 of her children and then did away with herself. The house where this supposedly happened is now gone. The area is still said to be haunted by Rhoda.

I've usually found that sensational stories such as this one have a small grain of truth. Now I would have to peel off the layers of folklore to get to the kernel.

The next part of Britany's story made my spider sense tingle. The haunted cemetery was a party spot for kids. The entity would be taunted by drunken teenagers and the cemetery was often trashed. If there was a presence in the area, its negativity could grow from the negativity brought by each group of trespassers.

I contacted Cindy to make arrangements to meet up with Britany to go to the cemetery. A couple of weeks later, Kim and I met with Britany and her friend, Anne Starr. After the introductions we followed the girls in our car out to the cemetery. A 10-minute drive brought us out in the middle of a huge corn field. A large wooded area was next to the rows of corn. The girls were right; without a guide you could be right next to the place and would never find it. Next to the cornfield we walked, cameras and meters at the ready. Suddenly Britany pointed to a small clearing through the trees. Even though it was early September I was glad I had worn long pants. Poison ivy and snakes were everywhere. After three minutes of watching every step we took, we came to the cemetery. It's hard to say how big the cemetery was because it was so very overgrown with vegetation.

Before we entered, we said a prayer of protection. Now that we were there, I wondered if it would be enough.

Britany was a photography student and she was armed with a camera beyond my comprehension. Anne would stay with her as lookout. Kim had our 35mm camera and I had the TriField Meter and thermo scanner. A thermo scanner measures ambient air temperature. It is often used in ghost hunting. It uses infared technology to test the air's temperature differences to detect any fluctuation. We decided to walk around the cemetery, take photos and gather information.

It was a bright Saturday afternoon. The temperature was about 77 degrees with not a cloud in the sky. Because the area was so old, we had a good-sized canopy of foliage over our heads.

Britany and Anne wandered off and Kim and I soon became separated. This happens all the

Investigating with detection devices in Rhoda's Cemetery

time. I was getting no readings from the equipment. I would just have to gather information.

I found Rhoda's headstone lying against the trunk of a tree. It had been broken off from its base. The headstone, as were all the others I came across, was made of sandstone. Because it had been lying at an angle, it was quite weathered. I was able to read:

Rhoda
Wife of John H. Galbreath
Born Dec 6, 1826
Died Apr. 4, 1876

Well, this shot down the Civil War suicide part of the story. There was also a hole next to the headstone. I was told it would never stay filled. It was full of beer cans when I was there. As a matter of fact, the entire cemetery was littered with beer cans and liquor bottles. Trash was strewn about and many of the headstones were toppled over. To see the cemetery in such a sad state was very disheartening.

Rhoda's grave was actually on the other side of the fallen tree that her headstone was resting on. I discovered this when I found the base to the headstone.

An hour had passed and it was now time for us to go. Comparing notes, we fount that the girls found nothing amiss. On the other hand, Kim was encountering all kinds of camera problems. The camera worked perfectly except for two places in the cemetery. Either the camera wouldn't work or it had a life of its own. This happens to her quite often, and I've learned to take it in stride.

I had just informed the others that I didn't know if anything was here or not when I buckled over from pain. It felt like a jolt of electricity shooting through my right arm and into my chest. The power of it was quite painful. While standing as erect as I could, I shouted at Kim to take some pictures. After only two photos I had to leave, the energy was that strong.

The trek out of the woods seemed to go much faster than the trek into the woods. At the safe haven of the cars, we discussed what had happened. I asked the girls to go home and write down their impressions of the day's events. I also wanted any photos of interest. We agreed to meet again in a couple of days.

It wasn't until we picked up our photos that I noticed the camera issues. All of Kim's photos that had been taken in two specific areas were distorted. It was even on the negative. The two areas were next to Rhoda's grave and thirty feet to the southwest. That spot contained several graves with broken headstones. Britany's pictures were more dramatic. In the same two locations in the cemetery, her shots contained a hovering mist. I was there and I know what the conditions were. The mist couldn't be explained by the warm temperature, low humidity or tricks of the sun.

Now it was back to Kim and I, as I had not formed my own group as yet. I

An unexplained mist that was not visible to the naked eye appeared in photographs that were taken at Rhoda's graveyard

have been fortunate over the years to meet some folks who have specialties in the field of the paranormal. The person I turned to this time was Barb Huyser. I met Barb during an American Ghost Society conference in Alton. She has a wonderful and soothing speaking voice that immediately fills you with a sense of trust. One of her specialties is cemeteries. I contacted Barb via e-mail and reintroduced myself. Besides hearing her speak at the conference, I also had purchased her book, "Small Town Ghosts." I was sure that she could help guide me through the investigation. I filled Barb in on all the details of my initial walkthrough. I gave her locations and events. Then I waited. Barb's response came later the same evening. She described three possible explanations for what might be happening:

1. Many cemeteries have intense activity during the initial phases of an investigation. After a period of time, the spirits are less interested in the ghost hunters, the novelty wears off.

2. An earthbound spirit, or spirits, in the area may have been responding to my interest. It isn't necessarily the case that the spirits are bound to the cemetery. They may be from the area and were attracted by my interest and my expressed intent to find spirits.

3. The spirits probably can't tell any difference between me and vandals at

first. Over time, as my energy becomes more familiar to them, I may feel more welcomed.

Barb then told me to take trash bags with me whenever I went back to show my respect for the area. Apparently, a little cleaning goes a long way with the spirits.

At this part of the e-mail response, it dawned on her that we were talking about a place that she was very familiar with. Back in 1977, Barb had been part of an investigation of the same cemetery. It just couldn't be a coincidence that we were joining forces to investigate the same spot. Barb promised to get back to me with more information. Her next dispatch blew me away.

When Barb found out that I was investigating the same cemetery, it scared the heck out of her. In Barb's own words, "My heart sank right to the pit of my stomach." Rhoda's house was the first truly major investigation that she was a part of. She told me that they made many mistakes and stirred up lots of negative energy. She also described feeling the energy the same way as I had: shooting right through her. It happened in the cemetery and in the house. This is the way Barb described her encounter:

Back in 1977, the cemetery was already completely overgrown and uncared-for. The cemetery was from the mid-1800s and the most recent burial was from the late 1800s. The house was almost in tumbledown condition. If it hadn't been built of brick, it would have been gone already. The front of the house faced the south with a generous front yard between it and the gravel road. There was a wide front door and the remains of a porch. Each of the rooms at the front of the house had tall, narrow windows. The doors and the windows were long gone.

The house was two stories with a wide hallway down the center on each floor and two rooms off each side of the hallway for a total of four rooms upstairs and four downstairs. The main stairway had a landing halfway up. There was a second stairway, which went from the main floor to the upstairs via the rooms in the northeast quadrant.

The wood floors were in bad shape, as were all the stairs. There were places where there were holes in the floor. It was quite unsafe to be in the building, though that didn't slow us idiots down much. Keep in mind, these were the days before EMF detectors or even the theory that ghosts and spirits were a form of electromagnetic energy. We really didn't have a handle on the quantum physics or the research methodology we have now. Our equipment consisted primarily of flashlights and tape recorders. We were too poor to have cameras or afford film and developing. In the '70s and before, pretty much everyone relied on psychic impressions.

The first time we went out was with an instructor from McKendree College, Dr. Bosse. She knew the history of the house and didn't tell us anything before we got there. We went through the house independently of each other and wrote down impressions. One member of the team who was sensitive picked up on the name Rhoda. I picked up on the name Sarah.

Both of us felt the narrow stairs going between the two back rooms was dangerous, like someone might reach out and trip us or give us a shove. We both felt the back bedroom in the northeast quadrant where those stairs were was uncomfortable.

The story Dr. Bosse related to us was that the house had been built before the Civil War. The original owners were Rhoda and her husband. They had a 12-year-old daughter, Sarah. At the time of the Civil War, Rhoda's husband went off to fight. While he was gone, Sarah died in a fall down the back stairs. There was speculation around town that Sarah was not Rhoda's husband's child. There had been gossip that Rhoda had an affair with her husband's best friend and that Sarah was a product of that relationship. Apparently, Rhoda's husband found this out not long before the Civil War started and it strained their marriage, possibly resulting in his enlisting to fight in the war.

This part is based on some of the information Dr. Bosse had, plus information we generated in the course of our investigation. I can't remember which was which any more. Dr. Bosse had been looking into the house and the haunting for at least a few years. She had learned about it through the college students who regularly went out there for thrills and drinking parties. Dr. Bosse was aware of incidents where students brought some items they found in the house back to the dorms at McKendree. Poltergeist activity ensued and did not stop until the items were returned to the house. There was also an incident Dr. Bosse was very alarmed about where a high school girl who claimed to be psychic experienced a personality change that lasted a few days after a visit to the house. Dr. Bosse was thoroughly convinced a genuine haunting was taking place.

During our investigation, we had some very strange stuff happen. That sense of energy passing through you was one a couple of us experienced, as well as cold blasts of air. We experienced this in the house as well as the cemetery. That back bedroom in the northeast quadrant of the upstairs had an absolute buzz of energy to it. There were times we'd take equipment into the house and it would stop working in that back bedroom. It would start working once we went back into the hallway.

We were dumb enough to bring a Ouija board out there. We first took it out to the cemetery where we believed we contacted Rhoda's husband. He "told" us that Rhoda was the powerful presence we felt and that Sarah was the weak presence. We suspected that Rhoda had knocked Sarah down the stairs in a fit of anger, blaming her for the estrangement with her husband. This could have completely out of our unconscious minds, having gone through a Ouija board, but the husband told us the same story.

Jo was the student on our team who was most strongly sensitive to spirits. She continually picked up on Rhoda and described her as malicious. If she did knock her daughter down the stairs, she wasn't the least bit repentant about it. I tended to pick up on Sarah. She was a weak presence, mostly found in the upstairs bedroom in the southeast quadrant of the house. She stood by the window and looked out of it most of time, looking for her father. There was a distinct cold spot by that window. What the father told us through the Ouija board was that Sarah was stuck there as long as Rhoda was present because he couldn't get through Rhoda to go get her and take her out of the house. He loved her, no matter what.

We went to the house several times. We got that EVP (electronic voice phenomenon) in the cemetery on the one occasion. Ultimately, we wanted to help Sarah but realized that we were in over our heads in trying to deal with Rhoda. Jo was becoming obsessed with the idea that if she could go to the house alone, she could deal with Rhoda. Given what happened to the high school girl, the team felt it was a phenomenally bad idea. We ended up quitting cold turkey with the investigation because we weren't getting anywhere and the house was getting more and more negative every time we went. I believe Rhoda was feeding off the attention and energy we brought with us, so she would do things to keep us coming back.

The local history told us that Rhoda was disliked by many people. She was bossy, nasty, judgmental of others, and hadn't lived an entirely pure life herself. There was even something on her tombstone about how she gave others advice (I wish I could remember the quote. It was kind of sarcastic.) Apparently, Rhoda and her husband got back together enough where they tolerated each other. There were some other children from the marriage.

Rhoda and her husband were buried in the cemetery, but we never found Sarah's grave. We wondered if the marker was worn away or buried under the brush somewhere.

We tried using the Ouija board on other investigations and could only ever get Rhoda on it. She wanted us to come back. We ended up having a little fire with that Ouija board to get rid of it.

I've often wondered about what happened to Sarah. I heard in the early 1980s that the house had been torn down due to the owners' concern about college students having beer busts out there. I don't blame them! I'm surprised no one fell through a floor and got hurt out there.

Sarah was only encountered in the house. Rhoda was encountered in the house and cemetery. I believe the voice we heard on the tape was actually Rhoda. She was saying exactly what would keep a bunch of psychology graduate students interested and coming out to the house on a regular basis. With the house gone, I hope Sarah was able to cross over.

If your cemetery is the same one, I suspect there is no coincidence there. I've always felt there was unfinished business since we could not rescue Sarah as long as Rhoda held her there. Rhoda, unrepentant and nasty, would still be there even if the house wasn't. Sarah might not even notice the house was gone. She was caught up in a pattern of continually waiting for her father and might be oblivious to the house being torn down. So, if it is the same cemetery, I suspect some guides have choreographed things for me to return. It would probably be spring before I could get there, but I would absolutely have to go. Maybe with the years of experience I've had since in dealing with entities, help from Amy Myers, and help from you, we might be able to rescue Sarah.

Good Lord, Len. Maybe I'm getting carried away by the possibility, but this could be really important. Please keep your friends away from there until we know for sure. It may take a daylight visit of you going out there and looking at the tombstones to see if you find Rhoda's. It is seductively active for ghost hunters and just as dangerous.

This kind of help was more than I could have hoped for!

In the beginning of this chapter brought up the fact that everything paranormal isn't a demon. Barb and I agree on this point. In regard to negative energies, we agree there are entities who are negative.

Some ghosts are extremely negative. Rhoda is a perfect example of this. In life, Rhoda hated people, was emotionally and physically abusive and most likely a murderer. They don't come much nastier than that. We also believe there are some entities who have never been human and can get into the mix at times. This is very rare.

If a person who has depression or other mental health issues lives in an area where one of these negative entities is around, they might be affected by it. Depression, substance abuse, mental illness, all these could be made worse through the influence of a negative entity.

Barb and I made a pact to meet in Lebanon the following spring to go to see what exactly Rhoda was up to. First, I wanted to map out the location. I waited for early November. The snakes and poison ivy would be gone and I could tread wherever I pleased. With me that Saturday afternoon were Kim, my friend Ernie, and his wife, Kim, and my other dear friend, Linda Kaegel. The air was cold and crisp and ,the sun was shining. What could go wrong?

After meeting at the Looking Glass Playhouse, we piled into my minivan and made our way to see Rhoda. I was hoping to map out the cemetery. I also wanted the girls to do headstone rubbings. I felt there had to be a ton of information just waiting to be copied. I don't know how many of you believe in omens but I started to notice that the closer we got to our destination, the darker and more overcast the sky suddenly became. After parking the car on the side of the road, I went to the house that was within 100 yards of the cemetery entrance. I wanted to know if it was their property and if it was all right for us to be there. No one was home so we decided to enter the cemetery.

The vibrant colors of the fall had given way to the drabness of winter. The leaves that were still on the trees were dried out and brown. This time our progress would be impeded, not by snakes and poison ivy, but by piles of dead leaves. Armed with paper and dark chalk, the two Kims and Linda started the headstone rubbings. I grabbed Ernie to help me determine the size of the cemetery. Our tools consisted of paper, pencils, a long tape measure and divining rods.

When I use divining rods, I'm looking for energy sources. I don't use them to ask questions or look for signs. They can easily be misused and misread. For whatever reason, I've had good luck measuring cemetery boundaries. Ernie and I were a good fifty yards from the girls when we stopped to get our bearings. The cemetery was turning out to be much larger than I anticipated. As leaves were brushed away, more and more headstones were coming to light.

Now I want to mention something that just occurred to me. This was my second visit to the site and I don't remember seeing or hearing a bird of any kind on either trip. The quiet was deafening.

With a creek in front of us, Ernie and I had no choice but to change directions. Sloshing through the dead leaves, I walked about forty feet before stopping. I stopped as I became aware that Ernie wasn't answering my questions. When I turned around, Ernie was still frozen to the spot by the creek. His jaw was dropped wide open. I asked him what the problem was. His reply was a trifle unique. I had gotten a 10-foot start on Ernie before he was ready to follow. On looking up, Ernie watched the leaves on the ground go up and down behind me. He also spotted a second set of foot imprints in the leaves. The prints were five feet to the side of me and three feet behind me. The prints were keeping pace with me. I had heard someone walking behind me and assumed that it was Ernie. Again, after examination, we could find no explanation. Ernie kept pace with me after that.

On returning to the girls, we found that they weren't having much luck. With the headstones being made of sandstone, they hadn't held up well. Also, when vandals had tipped over many of the headstones, which exposed them to rainfall and other weather elements.

It was now four in the afternoon and the sun would be setting soon, the little voices in our heads told us it was time to go, and quickly.

Early the next summer, Barb Huyser, Amy Myers and several cohorts met up with me in Lebanon. Barb informed me that Amy was a sensitive, not a psychic. This would be interesting...

We made our way to the cemetery. We were well armed with long pants, long sleeves and boots. The snakes and poison ivy would not stop us.

When Barb got out of the van, she was immediately transported back to 1977. She walked the field and pointed out where Rhoda's house had stood, as well as the summer kitchen, outhouse and barn. She told us again of her encounters there. The house was gone, but the cemetery awaited our arrival.

This is where Amy Myers started to dazzle me. Amy nailed all the spots in the cemetery where I had encountered unusual things. Amy described Rhoda and her daughter, Sarah. According to Amy, Sarah was being held to the site by Rhoda. The others were in total agreement with Amy's observation. I only knew that she verified my encounters.

The girls decided to do a spirit rescue of Sarah. I moved to the side and set up my video camera. Barb, Amy and the girls called on spirit guides and others to protect them from Rhoda and to allow Sarah to be free. They believed that Sarah was freed. The only unusual thing I experienced was a blast of icy cold air for about 30 seconds. This was in the middle of a hot June afternoon.

When the girls decided that Sarah was now free, it was time to go. Run is more of what we did. They all believed they could only keep Rhoda at bay for so long.

We went back to the theater so the girls could change into comfortable clothes. Flushed with victory, I decided to test Amy. I couldn't verify what happened at the cemetery. We were now in my theater. Under the guise of touring the grand old theater, I walked the group throughout the building. Amy was right behind me while we toured. This time she blew my mind with facts and happenings that only I could know. Amy stopped at every spot where I had encountered activity in the theater. She then proceeded to describe all three of the full-figure apparitions that I have come face-to-face with. Then she gave me messages from several of the entities. The messages were only for me and contained information that only I would know about. I was now a believer!

With total exhaustion upon us, we decided to do the cemetery next year to see if Rhoda was still around. Barb figured she may leave with no one to torment.

Before Barb and the girls came back the following year, I decided to try and dig up some more information on Rhoda. I spread the word through Lebanon that I wanted to find out how the legend began. Several months passed before I got a reply.

The man who contacted me was a guy that I've known for quite a while. To protect his identity we'll call him Carl. I sat down one Saturday afternoon in February and recorded Carl's story. Two hours and 12 beers later, I had some great tales to match up with Barb Huyser.

Carl said he started going to Rhoda's house in 1972. A Lebanon local, 15-year-old Carl had been working for a Lebanon farmer in the area near the cemetery and Rhoda's house. Day after day, Carl wondered why he didn't see anyone going in or out of the house. The house appeared solid. The fencing outside was as good as new. The farmer informed him that as far as he knew, the house was vacant.

In Lebanon in the early 1970s, the place to go on the weekend was Pizza Hut in neighboring O'Fallon. After pizza, you were on your own. One Saturday night, Carl told his buddy about Rhoda's house. Twenty minutes later found the boys on the front porch. The heavy oak front door squeaked noisily when it was opened. After a quick search the boys found that the house was indeed vacant. Except for a basement full of water, it looked as if the resident family had just picked up and left.

Behind the house were an outhouse and a summer kitchen to the northeast. Northeast of the summer kitchen was a barn that had been converted into a two-car garage. The family cemetery was in the woods to the left of the house.

According to Carl, the cemetery had been a partying spot for local youth for as long as could remember. The vandalism had been going on for quite some time. Carl and his friend, whom we'll call Roger, were very respectful of the cemetery. The boys felt there were places you just didn't mess with.

One summer evening found the boys wandering through the cemetery. Bathed in the light of the full moon, they were trying to figure out who was buried there. Both boys had already heard the story of Rhoda. They were told that she was a crazy woman and a social outcast who lived on the outskirts of town. One night in a fit of rage, she killed her illegitimate daughter, then herself. (You notice how the story had grown to 13 children by the time I heard it?) The boys noticed a large headstone lying against the trunk of a fallen tree. As they approached the headstone, Roger let out a scream. He had fallen into a hole next to the headstone. Panic set in as Carl pulled his friend to safety. After rescuing Roger, Carl poked a stick in the hole and found it was only 18 inches deep. Carl wanted to stick the needle in Roger for that one. The lateness of the evening and a sudden cold chill changed his mind.

Up to this point, all the partying in the area had been done in the cemetery.

That would soon change. Carl and Roger couldn't believe that no one had bothered the house. So they claimed it as theirs. The Saturday night trips to Pizza Hut now included a ghost story. The boys amazed their friends with ghostly tales of the property. Carl and Roger would convince their friends to meet them at the house. If they were late, their friends were told to go on in and wait. The boys would then drive like bats out of hell to the old house. The barn wasn't locked and they hid Carl's car inside. When their friends arrived,   with no car in sight, they would go into the house to wait, unaware that Carl and Roger were already there. During the investigations of the house the boys had found that all the ductwork led to the basement. It only took a handful of rocks dropped strategically through the vents by the boys from the second floor to send their friends screaming into the night. This was the beginning of the end for the old house.

Originally Carl and Roger had only wanted a hideout to drink a few beers and scare some girls. The beer part took care of itself. The ghost stories had to be invented. It wasn't long before the ghostly events happened without the boys help.

Carl told me of how he and Roger, after hiding their car, would sometimes see someone walking through the house by the second floor windows. On further inspection, no one was ever found.

One night as the boys hid upstairs with their pile of gravel for the vents, they heard footsteps ascending the staircase. The house may have been slowly wearing away, but the solid oak staircase was strong as the day it was built. Carl wondered who would come the house alone. Roger wondered who the heck was going to go check out who was on the staircase. Together, the boys warily made their way to the top of the stairs. Their flashlights revealed that they were quite alone.

In my earlier chats with Barb Huyser, she told me that she believes that Rhoda pushed her daughter down the back servants' staircase. Of course, she told the townspeople it was an accident. Carl had a very interesting story about the same staircase. According to Carl, the back servants' stairs were impassable. That is, you could go up, but not down. It didn't seem to matter what time of day or night it was. When the boys were upstairs and they decided to go down the back stairs, they could only get about two-thirds of the way down. Some force seemed to envelope them every time. The feelings of dread and confinement were so strong that the boys would run back up the steps, through the second floor hallway, and out down the main staircase.

The ghost stories, real or not, were growing at an alarming rate. As word of the haunted cemetery and house spread, more and more young people showed up with mischief on their minds. It didn't take long for the vandalism to spread to the house. Walls were spray-painted. Windows and doors were broken. The beautiful fence that surrounded the property was torn down and trampled. The house had become an eyesore.

One night, acting on a tip, Carl and Roger stayed home when the St. Clair Police showed up at Rhoda's house with a school bus. The bus wasn't for education:

it was there to haul the mob of young, drunken vandals to jail. Because of the police intervention, the drunken orgies of destruction came to a close. But the damage was done. Alone and crippled, the house awaited its end. This is how the house came to be in the state it was in when Barb Huyser first saw it in 1977.

In 1977, Carl married a local girl. He still lives in Lebanon today. Roger got a job with the railroad and his whereabouts are unknown. During a second interview with Carl, he filled me in on a few more details about the house.

Different local groups, especially the Jaycees, talked about running a haunted house at the site but no one ever followed through on the idea. In the 1990s, the property owner had all the buildings razed. The owner feared kids breaking in and getting hurt. A track hoe came in, dug several holes, and buried everything. I saved all of this information for Barb.

The following June I met Barb, Amy, and the girls at the theater in Lebanon. We again made our way out to the cemetery. The sun was shining and it was quite hot. As I pulled into the driveway to the east of the old house, Barb literally jumped out the van and stood in front of the van with her arms outstretched. When I asked the girls what was happening, they told me that it felt like being at home! Barb jumped back into the van and showed me where to park. As we exited the van, she told us to hurry as we only had a small window of opportunity. I wanted to ask her about that opportunity, but I was told to be quiet.

I led the girls into the woods, recording everything with my video camera. This was no time to worry about snakes and poison ivy. I realized that while the girls were doing a quick prayer of protection, I was getting the gear from the van. I was low man on the totem pole again! The deeper into the woods we went, the mote the stillness enveloped us. By the time we stood in the middle of the cemetery, facing Rhoda's grave, it was as if we were in a tomb, the quiet was deafening.

Barb finally gave us the information we craved. She believes that she has had a connection with Rhoda since 1977. Barb refers to herself as a paranormal social worker. Rhoda just happened to be her toughest case. Barb reminds me a lot of my wife. I believe they are sensitives who stifle their gifts. If they let it fly and develop it (and I believe Barb is now doing that), they might be half as good as Amy Myers. Barb felt that Rhoda was with us, but in a seriously weakened state. With Sarah freed the year before, she had no one to dominate. This caused her to gradually weaken.

Barb, Amy and the girls did a rescue operation on Rhoda. I did what I do best: I got out of the way and filmed. They called on spirit guides and angels and anyone else who would listen. After 20 minutes, they told me that Rhoda had passed over. Being as psychic as a brick, I had no way of knowing if this were true or not. I did notice one unusual thing, though: I could hear the birds. That was the first time in all of my trips to the cemetery that birds had been audible. The air, though still hot, felt lighter. Something had happened. I just wasn't certain what.

In 2007, Barb, Amy and I made one last trip to the cemetery. The late June morning was warm, yet comfortable. As we stood by Rhoda's headstone, I pointed out that we could still hear the birds chirping. It was definitely a good sign!

As our perfect morning was coming to a close, loud crashing footsteps raced up behind us. I honestly thought Rhoda was giving us one last shot. To our surprise, and relief, it was a golden lab. Twenty feet behind the dog was a lady with a questioning look on her face.

After removing the dog from my crotch, I went over to the lady and introduced myself and told her what we were doing. She told us that she lived in the house next door and that the cemetery was part of her property. That was why she was checking on us. Although the kids weren't as bad as they used to be, she still got an idiot or two out there every now and then.

I let her know that we had tried previously to ask permission to visit the cemetery, never finding anyone at home. I then introduced Barb and Amy. The lady bore us no ill will for our presence that morning. She seemed happy that instead of drunken teenagers, some intelligent folks came by for a visit. She felt that way towards the girls. The jury was still out on me.

It was now time to go on our merry way. While shaking the owner's hand with my right hand, and fending off the dog with my left, I bid her goodbye. She grasped my hand even tighter and asked, "What was your name again?" I responded, "Len Adams." A smile crossed her face as she told me that she had one of my business cards. It seems that her daughter, Libby, had worked with me on a tour in Alton. Libby came to my rescue when I found that I had a tour for a group of deaf folks coming to Alton. I found Libby through a local college to sign to these folks. I now have a standing invitation to visit the site in the future.

With our goodbyes renewed, the girls and I made our way home. I have rarely visited the cemetery since that beautiful June morning. I am usually alone and alone is not what you want to be in the middle of the woods. I don't know if Barb, Amy and the girls freed Sarah and Rhoda. Barb and Amy have become very dear friends of mine. If they believe it happened, that's good enough for me. I do know the place has a different feel, a good vibe you might say.

To this day, kids from Summerfield, Mascoutah, Lebanon and all around the area still tell the legend of Rhoda. Remember that most stories, no matter how outlandish, have a kernel of truth. Your job, if you accept it, is to peel back the layers and find that kernel.

Happy Hauntings to you all!

AFTERWORD

I hope you've enjoyed your trek through a place I dearly love. This book was one of the hardest things I've ever done because of my emotional bond with the players and places involved.

If you were looking for clear-cut answers as to why a place is haunted or not, you won't find them here. The more research I do on the topic of the paranormal, the less I am sure as to why these things happen. There are patterns, but no hardcore facts.

If you wish to visit some of these locations, and I hope you come to see me on a tour, be respectful of the living, as well as the dead.

1. Do not force your way into a location. Just because you tell someone you're a ghost hunter doesn't make you a legitimate paranormal investigator.

2. Don't monopolize a shopkeeper's time. Selling their wares to the living is their main concern.

3. DO NOT TRESPASS! I cannot stress this enough. You will, and rightly so, go to jail for intruding where you are not welcome. Remember, we are like vampires. We only come in when we are invited.

4. If you come on a tour of Lebanon, relax. I know you want to see a ghost but I can't promise that something will happen. I can only promise that a location might have the law of averages working in our favor, nothing else. If you go anywhere on a ghost tour and are promised definite action or photos, you are being deceived.

5. A person is not psychic just because they tell you they are. For every person I've come across with real abilities, I've had to put up with 50 fakes.

I honestly believe we all have the ability to move the spectral veil aside and experience what's behind the curtain. Some people are more gifted than others. It always fascinated me why animals and children seem to have many ghostly encounters. Then I realize that the children haven't been taught to put the walls of denial in front of them, like many adults have. Animals just see things as they really are.

BIBLIOGRAPHY

Brink, McDonough & Co., History of St. Clair County, 1881, 1977 Centennial McKendree History, 1928

Church, H.V., Illinois, History-Geography-Government Lebanon Centennial Commission, 1974, History in a Nutshell

Monroe, Dona, A History of The Looking Glass Playhouse, 1972-1990

Perrin, Nick J., Perrins History of Illinois

St. Clair County Bicentennial Commission, Tapestry of Time, 1790-1990

St. Clair County Genealogical Society, 1988, History of St. Clair County, IL.

St. Clair County Genealogical Society, History of St. Clair County, IL., Vol. II, 1992

St. Clair County Genealogical Society, 1994, 1890 Census Substitute of St. Clair County

Taylor, Troy & Adams, Len -- So There I was, More Confessions of Ghost Hunters (2006)

Taylor, Troy -- The Ghost Hunters Guidebook (2007)

The Lebanon History Book Committee, A Reminiscent View of Lebanon, Illinois, 1998

The Pictorial Book Committee of Lebanon, A Pictorial View of Historic Lebanon, Illinois, 1996

Personal Interviews & Correspondence

Special Thanks to:
Jill Hand - Editing & Proofreading Services
John Brill
Don Urban
Harrison Church

Troy Taylor
Ernie Lingo
Linda Kaegal
Luke Naliborski
Janet Scmitt
Rick Schmitt
Kathy Heberts
Jo Turk
Sarah Ruth
Pat Peterson
Bill Alsing
Lebanon Historical Society
& Kim Adams

ABOUT THE AUTHOR

Len Adams is the Vice-President of The American Ghost Society and lead guide for Troy Taylor's Alton Hauntings Tours in Southwestern Illinois. Len is also the creator (and only tour guide) of the Haunted Lebanon Tours in Lebanon, Ill. He has been actively investigating the paranormal for many years and currently handles the AGS investigations for most of downstate Illinois. This is his second book.

Adams has been hosting ghost tours in Alton and Lebanon for several years, as well as haunted overnights in Southern Illinois, and has also appeared in a number of newspaper articles about ghosts and hauntings. He has been interviewed numerous times for radio and television broadcasts about the paranormal and has been featured for several local news broadcasts. Adams has also been a featured paranormal expert on several episodes of "Cringe," produced by Troy Taylor. He has also served as a public speaker for private and public groups in St. Louis and the surrounding area.

Born in St. Louis and raised in southern Illinois, Len resides in Belleville with his wife, Kim. His current home is "ghost free," but, as he says-----"there's always hope."

HAUNTED LEBANON GHOST TOURS

HISTORY AND HAUNTINGS OF THE LOOKING GLASS PRAIRIE

Join the Illinois Hauntings Tours & Len Adams for a historic and frightening tour through one of Southern Illinois' most beautiful, and haunted, small towns. Lebanon was founded in 1804 but the culture here dates back to pre-history, as evidence by Emerald Mound, located just outside of town. Lebanon is also home to Illinois' oldest college, McKendree, which was founded in 1824. Charles Dickens, during his travels in America, stopped in Lebanon in 1842 while visiting the Looking Glass Prairie. The Mermaid Inn, built in 1830, served as his stopover point on his journey west. Lebanon's main street stands alone as a ghost hunters' paradise. From mysterious underground tunnels to phone calls from the beyond, you'll jump between the present and the past, the living and the dead with this chilling tour! Based on Len Adams' book, **Phantoms in the Looking Glass**, the Haunted Lebanon tour is a 3-hour walking tour & spine tingling journey into the haunted history of Lebanon.

AVAILABLE APRIL THRU OCTOBER!

CALL 1 888 446 7859 FOR RESERVATIONS AND FIND OUT ABOUT PRIVATE TOURS AND DINNER TOURS FOR GROUPS!

CPSIA information can be obtained at www.ICGtesting.com
Printed in the USA
LVOW05s0004230814

400325LV00002B/9/P